CONVAIR

Martyn Chorlton

AMBERLEY

First published 2018

Amberley Publishing
The Hill, Stroud, Gloucestershire, GL5 4EP
www.amberley-books.com

Copyright © Martyn Chorlton, 2018

The right of Martyn Chorlton to be identified as the
Author of this work has been asserted in accordance with
the Copyright, Designs and Patents Act 1988.

ISBN 978 1 4456 8087 3 (print)
ISBN 978 1 4456 8088 0 (ebook)

British Library Cataloguing in Publication Data.
A catalogue record for this book is available from the
British Library.

Origination by Amberley Publishing.
Printed in Great Britain.

Contents

Introduction

Every aircraft ever built has a manufacturer behind it and, just like a family tree, those companies that have not folded over the years can be traced back in time to at least one group that still exists today. Convair is no exception; today it exists in spirit as part of the history of General Dynamics, which was formed in 1952, two years before the term 'Convair' was officially recognised instead of its original full title, 'Consolidated-Vultee'. Between 1953 and 1954 General Dynamics acquired Convair, although the name remained until 1996. Our story begins on 17 March 1943 when the Consolidated Aircraft Corporation merged with Vultee Aircraft Inc., continuing to build some of the world's most incredible aircraft until 1964 and then taking part in the US space programme and producing a successful line of rockets and missiles, a process beginning in 1946 and culminating in the AGM-129 ACM cruise missile, which entered service in 1990.

The Convair Family

The Consolidated Element

The Consolidated Aircraft Corporation was founded by Major Reuben H. Fleet in 1923. Born in Montesano, Washington, on 6 March 1887, Fleet had a good start in life thanks to his father, David. He was a city engineer and county auditor of Montesano who had acquired large areas of land in Washington Territory. Fleet joined Culver Military Academy at the age of fifteen and then trained as a teacher but in 1907 he decided that real estate was his future and, within twelve months, was investing heavily thanks to a loan from Montesano State Bank. A captain in a National Guard company by 1911, Fleet closed down his real estate office in 1917 and was commissioned as a major in the US Army. He later graduated as a Junior Military Aviator (Licence No. 74).

Located in Buffalo, New York, the corporation came about due to the liquidation of the Gallaudet Aircraft Company and the closure of the Dayton-Wright Company, which was being shut down by its parent company, General Motors. Fleet worked for Gallaudet and in 1923 he decided to form his own company, Consolidated. A number of Dayton-Wright designs were purchased in the deal; the first of them was the PT-1 Trusty trainer designed by Colonel Virginius Clark, who was also the Vice President

Reuben Hollis Fleet (1887–1975), the founding father of Consolidated. (*Richard Ward Collection*)

of Consolidated. The NY and PT-3 trainers followed, with the O-17 Courier, the Fleetster and the impressive Commodore flying boat in 1930. The knowledge gained from the Commodore and the later P2Y for the US Navy would lead to the first really big success for Consolidated, the outstanding Catalina. Further success would follow in the shape of the B-24 Liberator which, alongside the B-17 Flying Fortress, would become the mainstay of the USAAF bomber force in multiple theatres during the Second World War.

Above: One of Consolidated's early aircraft designs was the PT-3 two-seat primary trainer. 130 PT-3s served the USAAC during the late 1920s and 1930s. (*Richard Ward Collection*)

Below: Another hugely successful military machine from the Consolidated stable was the PBY Catalina, which was one of the most commonly sighted, and often most welcome, flying boats of the Second World War. It also enjoyed a lengthy post-war military career that did not end until 1979! This example is the sole XPBY-5A, 1245, which was introduced into service from late 1940. (*Richard Ward Collection*)

Another classic from Consolidated was the B-24 Liberator, which alongside the B-17 (and often in the shadow of it) provided the backbone of the USAAF bomber campaign across all theatres of the Second World War. Over 19,000 were built by Consolidated, Douglas Ford and North American in five factories across the States. (*Richard Ward Collection*)

By 1941, Consolidated became the largest employer in San Diego, but in November of that same year Fleet decided to bow out. He sold his shares in Consolidated for $10.9 million to the President of AVCO (Aviation Corporation), Victor Emanuel, under the proviso that Consolidated and Vultee (already a subsidiary of AVCO) would be merged. This duly took place in 1943 and the company became Consolidated-Vultee.

The Vultee Element

The roots of Vultee go back to early 1932, when Gerard 'Jerry' Freebairn Vultee and Vance Breese created the Airplane Development Company (ADC) in response to interest being shown by American Airlines in one of their aircraft designs. This aircraft was the attractive V-1 single-engined airliner. Not long after, the American businessman Errett Lobban 'E. L.' Cord purchased all 500 shares of the ADC, which meant that the new company became a subsidiary of the Cord Corporation. It was no coincidence that other Cord holdings included Lycoming Engines, the Stinson Aircraft Company and American Airlines. By 1934, AVCO had created the Aviation Manufacturing Corporation (AMC) and purchased a number of Cord holdings in late 1934, including the now more formally named Vultee Airplane Development Corporation. By early 1936, the AMC had been liquidated but this meant that Vultee became more established as a subsidiary of AVCO. By this time, 'Jerry' Vultee had been appointed as Vice President and Chief Engineer while the company grew in strength thanks to the acquisition of Lycoming and Stinson.

In the meantime, work continued on the V-1 airliner, which had evolved into an eight-seat production machine designated the V-1A, specifically for the needs of American Airlines. American would only purchase eleven V-1s in the end from a total production output of twenty-five aircraft, including the prototype. The V-1 was also being developed into a military variant, the V-11 attack aircraft, which was considerably more successful and 224 were built. In 1937, 'Jerry' Vultee was in charge of his factory at Downey, California, and the future looked bright. Sadly, Vultee and his wife, Sylvia Parker, were killed in a plane crash near Sedona, Arizona, on 29 January 1938.

Dick Palmer took over the reins from Vultee when the company began to focus more on military aircraft such as the BT-13 family of trainers and the Model V-72 Vengeance dive bomber. In November 1939, Vultee finally stood alone as an independent company, by then officially known as the Vultee Aircraft Division. Further military designs included the moderately successful P-66 Vanguard and the impressive looking XP-54 'Swoose Goose' fighter.

In March 1943, as designed by Reuben H. Fleet, Consolidated and Vultee merged and the rest, as they say, is history.

Gerald 'Jerry' Freebairn Vultee (1900–38), a gifted engineer whose life was sadly cut short in a plane crash in January 1938. (*Richard Ward Collection*)

One of Vultee's great successes was their range of training aircraft, which included the BT-13A Valiant. Used by the US Army, Navy and Air Force and a host of overseas operators, 6,407 BT-13As were built. (*Richard Ward Collection*)

Above: The Vultee A-31 Vengeance was intended as a dive bomber in US operational service but instead found favour in the hands of the RAF, RAAF and IAF in the Far East during the Second World War. (*Richard Ward Collection*)

Below: Just five years after the end of the Second World War, Convair could boast a wide and diverse range of military aircraft including the XFY-1 Pogo VTOL fighter, XF2Y-1 Sea Dart naval fighter, RB-36 Peacemaker long-range bomber, R3Y Tradewind cargo flying boat and YF-102 fighter. Only two of these amazing machines would result in a significant production contract. (*Convair/Richard Ward Collection*)

Right: The 'Sound of Freedom' was a common term associated with all Cold War fighters and the dramatic and exciting F-102 Delta Dagger was no exception. An aircraft that represented the aerial defence of the USA, the F-102 served from 1956 through to 1979. (*Convair/Richard Ward Collection*)

Below: A wonderful design from front to back, the Convair 880 was sadly a total failure from a sales point of view. Still one of the most attractive airliners ever built, the 880 may have been fast but it lacked the passenger-carrying capacity that so many airlines craved. (*Delta Airlines/ Richard Ward Collection*)

Convair created a number of amazing aircraft designs during its comparatively short existence and many books have been, and are still being, written about this period. This is an artist's impression of the XB-53 medium bomber, which was cancelled in 1949. (*Convair/Richard Ward Collection*)

XA-41

As would be expected in the middle of a world conflict, before their amalgamation both Consolidated and Vultee were already working on a number of projects but the first to be presented as a Convair project was the XA-41. Vultee took up the challenge in response to a USAAF remit which had been laid down in mid-1942 for a single-seat dive bomber. On 10 November 1942, a contract for a pair of prototype aircraft was issued to Vultee, who designated the machine the XA-41. However, as is the way with an air force during a complex multi-theatre war, the USAAF decided it no longer needed a new dive bomber and instead modified the contract in favour of a low-level ground attack machine. Understandably, Vultee needed some time to re-design the XA-41 and it was not until 10 April 1943 that a second, fully revised contract was issued for two aircraft to be serialled 43-35124 and 43-35125. The time had, by then, reached the point of the formation of Convair and, while still designated the XA-41, behind closed doors the aircraft was officially designated the Convair Model 90.

The USAAF changed its mind again in September 1943, to the point where it looked very much like the XA-41 was doomed. The P-47, P-51 and F4U Corsair, to name a few, were already performing well in the ground attack role and the USAAF saw little need for a new type. The first prototype was already close to being completed and, instead of 'canning' the exercise completely, the USAAF asked for one aircraft which could be used as a test bed for the Pratt & Whitney R-4360 engine. This was made official on 20 November 1943 but Convair still felt that it could make the XA-41 an attractive proposition to the USAAF as a long range fighter rather than a sterile test bed. However, the powers that be decided that the aircraft that were already in service were fulfilling their roles adequately and no further interest in the XA-41 as a pure military machine was shown.

The XA-41 was a big aircraft with a 54-foot wing span and a fuselage 48 feet 8 inches long. The first machine to be redesignated from its Vultee roots to a Convair aircraft, the XA-41 could not hide its Vultee dive-bomber heritage. (*Richard Ward Collection*)

The XA-41 was a low-wing cantilever monoplane with an oval-shaped fuselage and a retractable tailwheel. The fuselage was deep enough to allow for a large internal bomb bay while the main undercarriage units, attached to the forward edges of the inner wings, fully retracted into the leading edges of the wings, which made the XA-41 a very clean and potentially high-performing aircraft. This big single-seat aircraft had a bubble canopy and the outer wing sections had a dihedral of 8 degrees which gave the aircraft a purposeful appearance.

The sole prototype, 45-35124, carried out its maiden flight from March Field, California, on 11 February 1944. Despatched to Eglin Field, Florida, for evaluation by the USAAF, at low altitude the XA-41 was found to be highly manoeuvrable, but the military were not for turning and, by this time, twin-engined aircraft such as the A-26 were in vogue as ground attack machines. The XA-41 was also evaluated by the US Navy at Patuxent River, Maryland, before being transferred to Pratt & Whitney for test bed and trial work. Later, Pratt & Whitney bought the XA-41 outright and it was given the civilian registration NX60373. This was to be short-lived as the aircraft was scrapped in 1950 at Hartford, Connecticut.

The sole prototype XA-41 during early engine testing of the aircraft's R-4360-9 Wasp Major radial. (*Convair/Richard Ward Collection*)

Further engine testing, before the XA-41's maiden flight from March Field, California, on 11 February 1944. (*Convair/ Richard Ward Collection*)

XP-81

Designed by Charles R. 'Jack' Irvine and Frank W. Davis, who were Vultee's Chief Designer and Chief Test Pilot respectively, the XP-81 was a mixed-power fighter designed specifically for long range duties across the Pacific. In 1943, the USAAF was looking for ideas to improve the endurance and performance of long range fighters and a requirement for a turboprop engine and turbojet-powered aircraft was issued. A range of at least 1,250 miles and a maximum speed of 500 mph were two of the minimum requirements.

Irvine and Davis drew up an all-metal, low-wing cantilever monoplane installed with a TG-100 turboprop for the cruise, backed up by a 3,750 lb J33-GE-5 turbojet which could be fired up for take-off and high-speed flight. The TG-100 had an exhaust at the extreme tail of the aircraft while the intakes for the J33 would be mounted on the upper mid-fuselage. The XP-81 also had a fully pressurised cockpit and a tricycle undercarriage. Officially designated by Convair as the Model 102, work began in the drawing room on 5 January 1944, by which time the USAAF designation of XP-81 was in place and two prototypes were ordered with the serials 44-91000 and 44-91001. The original contract was later modified to include thirteen service aircraft for trial use to be known as the YP-81. The YP-81 was to be powered by the TG-110 turboprop, which was lighter and more powerful than the TG-100 which, combined with a full armament of six 0.5 in. machine guns or six 20 mm cannon, would have resulted in the wing being moved aft by 10 inches to compensate for the change in the centre of gravity.

The sole Convair XP-81, serialled 44-91000, prior to its maiden flight on 11 February 1945. Note the full company name at the time, 'Consolidated Vultee', on the nose while the unofficial title (at that time) of 'Convair' is displayed on the fin. (*Convair/Richard Ward Collection*)

A hybrid bird would be the best way of describing the XP-81, which had a General Electric XT31-GE-1 (TG-100) turboprop conventionally mounted in the nose and an Allison J33-GE-5 turbojet buried in the rear fuselage. The only indication of the latter from this angle is the two dorsal positioned air intakes. (*USAF Photo/Richard Ward Collection*)

By the time the airframe of 44-91000 was completed, the development of the TG-100 turboprop was lagging behind and, to keep the flight programme on track, a Packard-Merlin V-1560-7 from a P-51D was installed instead, complete with a P-38J-type radiator inlet below the hub of the propeller. After being taken by road to Muroc Dry Lake, XP-81 44-91000 made its maiden flight on 11 February 1945. The XP-81 handled reasonably well but an improvement in stability was needed and this was cured through extending the fin by 15 inches and adding a ventral fin.

Due to events occurring in the Pacific, the need for long range fighters had diminished and on 15 August 1945 (VJ Day) the order for the thirteen YP-81s was cancelled. The contract appeared to still stand for the two XP-81s and the first was flown back to Vultee Field under Merlin power in readiness for the installation of the intended TG-100 turboprop. 44-91000 made its first flight under turboprop power on 21 December 1945, a flight that proved to be disappointing as the unit only delivered 60 per cent of its potential power and was therefore no better than the Merlin it replaced! On 9 May 1947, the XP-81 programme was shut down and by the following year the two prototypes had been re-designated as the ZXF-81, which would indicate that their future lay in test and trial work. This did not materialise and in 1949 the two aircraft were taken to a bombing range at Edwards AFB. At least one, if not both, airframes were later recovered from the range and today components are in storage at the USAF Museum at Wright-Patterson AFB.

The tail pipe of the XP-81's J33 turbojet is visible from this angle, as is the ventral fin (just forward of the main undercarriage) which was installed following earlier instability issues. (*Convair/Richard Ward Collection*)

A heat trail from the J33 turbojet can be just seen as 44-9100 poses for the camera (at speed) during flight testing out of Edwards AFB, most likely around 1946. (*USAF Photo/Richard Ward Collection*)

L-13 'Grasshopper'

One of the companies under the Convair umbrella was the light aircraft manufacturer Stinson, which would remain a subsidiary until it was sold to Piper in 1950. One of the aircraft designed by Stinson during the Convair years was the L-13, a three-seat general purpose high-wing monoplane capable of carrying out medivac, liaison, observation or photographic roles.

The all-metal L-13's high wing was braced and foldable and featured leading-edge slats and slotted trailing edge flaps which gave the little aircraft excellent short-field and low-speed handling. A braced tailplane was mounted halfway up the fin and the fixed undercarriage could be fitted with floats or skis. The cabin was large enough for three crew in normal configuration although room could be made for a pair of stretchers with two crew and, in an emergency, up to six could be carried.

A pair of prototypes was ordered in 1945, given the designation XL-13 and serialled 45-58708 and 45-58709. A long and arduous test programme resulted in a contract for 300 aircraft in two batches of 146 (46-68 to 48-213) and 154 (47-267 to 47-420), with deliveries beginning with the Air National Guard in 1947. Shrewdly, Convair did not include the rights to the L-13 when Stinson was sold to Piper and, as such, all production was carried out by Convair.

A number of L-13As were converted for use in the Arctic and these were designated the L-13B; the conversion included skis and the fitment of a combustion heater. The bulk of the L-13As served with the USAF during the 1950s and into the early 1960s, although forty-three were transferred to the US Army at the beginning of the Korean War, in order to release more aircraft for service in that theatre.

Left: The prototype Convair XL-13, 45-58708, is presented with its main wings folding along the side of the rear fuselage and the tailplane folded to the near vertical. (*Convair/Richard Ward Collection*)

Right: Both prototype Convair XL-13s were painted in a US Army olive drab colour, including 45-58708, pictured during the 'long and arduous test programme'. (*Convair/Richard Ward Collection*)

B-36A Peacemaker

The seed for the world's first intercontinental bomber was sown as early as 11 April 1941, when a specification was issued for an aircraft capable of carrying a 72,000 lb bomb load. On top of that, and in light of the perilous situation Great Britain had found itself in at the time, the specification required the added capability to deliver a 10,000 lb bomb load on targets in Europe from stations located in the United States. Other details of the specification, in order to carry out such a long range mission, were the ability to fly a distance of 10,000 miles without refuelling at a maximum speed range of between 240 and 300 mph and to be able to operate at 35,000 ft.

This is an impressive and ambitious specification even today but Convair was up for the challenge and their Model 36 was selected out of four competing designs. The key features of the Model 36 were its long, pressurised fuselage and 230-foot wings which were 6 feet thick at the root, giving enough room for full in-flight access to the bomber's six pusher engines. This huge aircraft was initially designed with a pair of fins and rudders but these were eradicated before the prototype, designated the XB-36, was rolled out at Fort Worth on 8 September 1945. Serialled 42-13570, the XB-36 first took to the air on 8 August 1946 in the hands of Beryl Erickson and Gus Green. While the general configuration of the prototype would be similar to production aircraft, the XB-36 differed in having huge 110-inch diameter single main wheels and, more obviously, a blended cockpit which featured only a small step between the forward glass panels and the nose. The undercarriage was replaced with the production four-wheel main undercarriage bogie units on the second prototype, designated the YB-36 and serialled 42-13571, and which later also featured the more familiar raised cockpit arrangement. With the latter modification, the aircraft was re-designated as the YB-36A.

The prototype XB-36 lifts into the air from Fort Worth with Beryl Erickson at the controls. Note the differences between this and the later production machines, such as the 110-inch diameter main wheels and the different cockpit configuration. (*Convair/Richard Ward Collection*)

For those who have no idea what 110 inches (9 feet 1.6 inches (2.79 m)) looks like, this willing volunteer provides some scale to the largest aircraft tyre ever produced. (*Convair/Richard Ward Collection*)

The incredible sound and sheer presence of the XB-36 meant it certainly deserved its name of 'Peacemaker' and the more sinister 'Aluminium Overcast' or 'Magnesium Overcast'. (*Convair/Richard Ward Collection*)

The prototype XB-36 carried out a trial utilising tracked undercarriage units in 1950; the idea was not pursued! (*Convair/Richard Ward Collection*)

19

In the meantime, an order was placed on 23 July 1943 for 100 aircraft which would become the production B-36A. However, the war began to turn against the Germans during this time and Consolidated-Vultee quite rightly focussed the bulk of their attention on producing the B-24 Liberator and, as a result, the first production B-36A, 44-92004, did not make its maiden flight until 28 August 1947. Only twenty-two B-36As were built and these only served as armed crew trainers. The first of these machines was delivered to the 7th BW (Heavy) at nearby Carswell AFB on 26 June 1948.

It had already been decided that the production B-36s would have an impressive defensive armament of sixteen 20 mm cannon, although these were not installed in the B-36A. They were, however, introduced with the B-36B, of which seventy-three were built. With more power from its six R-4360 engines and a higher operating weight of 328,000 lb, the B-36B was the first serious variant to enter operational service. It first flew on 8 July 1948 and was again assigned to the 7th BW from November 1948. The defensive armament comprised six retractable and remotely controlled turrets in the fuselage, each fitted with a pair of 20 mm cannon, and two further pairs of 20 mm cannon mounted in the nose and tail.

The first production Convair B-36A-1-CF Peacemaker, 44-92004, possibly during, or not long after, its maiden flight on 28 August 1947. (*USAF/Richard Ward Collection*)

B-36B-1-CF 44-92027 in the foreground, in company with 44-92035 beyond, of the 26th BS, 7th BW, at Carswell AFB. 44-92035 was destined to crash near Cleburne, Texas, on 22 November 1950 with only two of the sixteen crew surviving. (*Life/Richard Ward Collection*)

The functional and, on first impression, roomy cockpit of a B-36 (at least a 'D' or retrofitted 'B' model; note the jet levers on the overhead panel), although the uninitiated would most likely change their opinion after a twenty-hour sortie! (*Convair/Richard Ward Collection*)

A proposed B-36C remained just that and never left the drawing board, while the B-36D was the next production variant. First flown on 29 March 1949, the first B-36D, 44-92057, was a conversion of a B-36B and was cleared to operate at 358,000 lb, which gave a potential full bomb load capacity of 84,000 lb. In addition to these impressive figures, the maximum speed rose to 435 mph and the ceiling was raised to over 45,000 ft thanks, in part, to the addition of two pairs of General Electric turbojets mounted underneath each outer wing section. Eighty-two B-36Ds were built, although sixty-four of this batch were actually B-36B conversions. With regard to the turbojets, the very first B-36D was installed with the J35 turbojet while the remainder were fitted with the J47-GE-19, each rated at 5,200 lb of thrust. The B-36D first entered service with the USAF's 7th BW on 19 August 1950. A sub-variant of the B-36D was the strategic reconnaissance RB-36D, of which seventeen were new builds and seven were B-36B conversions. The RB-36D had a crew complement of twenty-two (which included five gunners) and was equipped with fourteen K-17C, K-22A, K-38 and K-40 cameras installed within two of four bomb bays. The RB-36D entered service on 3 June 1950 with the 28th SRG at Rapid City, although, due to equipment and material shortages, the aircraft did not become operational until June 1951.

Built as a B-36B-10-CF, 44-92057 is seen after conversion to the prototype B-36D complete with a quartet of Allison J35-A-19 jets. In this configuration the aircraft made its maiden flight on 26 March 1949. (*Convair/ Richard Ward Collection*)

RB-36E 49-2020 'X' was originally built as a B-36A before conversion. This machine is pictured in service with the 5th SRW, 15th Air Force, operating out of Travis AFB, California. (*USAF/Richard Ward Collection*)

The 'E' variant was another strategic reconnaissance machine in the shape of the RB-36E, which was similar in all aspects to the RB-36D. The YB-36A and twenty-one B-36As were converted to RB-36E standard, the first of them flying on 18 December 1949 while the last conversion was completed by July 1951.

The next major variant was the B-36F, which mainly differed from its predecessors in having more powerful R-4360-53 engines. An improved radar and ECM equipment were also installed. The first of fifty-eight B-36Fs made its maiden flight on 18 November 1950 and the type was accepted into USAF service from March 1951. Of the production run, twenty-four aircraft were built as RB-36Fs, which were very similar to the RB-36D but featured a much improved defensive fire control system. A number of RB-36Fs were reconfigured to a more offensive combat role during the latter stages of their careers as more effective reconnaissance aircraft entered service.

A single RB-36F, 49-2707, had an interesting side career as part of the FICON (Fighter Conveyor) project, which successfully explored the concept of a bomber carrying a fighter or reconnaissance aircraft to extend its range and operating area. The B-36 was heavily converted, complete with a large cradle below the fuselage to carry a modified F-84E Thunderjet. Flight testing began in January 1952 and subsequently 170 in-flight launches and recoveries were carried out between the two aircraft. Following the success of these trials, eleven B-36s were converted and re-designated as the GRB-36D to serve with the 99th SRW at Fairchild. By 1956, the need for such a combination passed into history with the introduction into service of the long-range, high-flying Lockheed U-2.

B-36F-1-CF 49-2677 was converted to carry the main fuselage and delta wing of an XB-58 for aerodynamic testing. (*USAF/Richard Ward Collection*)

No fewer than eighteen B-36s were seriously damaged when a tornado swept through Carswell AFB on 1 September 1952. One of the aircraft recognisable in this scene is B-36F-1-CF 49-2675 'U'; the aircraft was not repaired. (*Richard Ward Collection*)

Eleven B-36s were converted to FICON (Fighter Conveyor) standard to serve with the 99th SRW at Fairchild AFB. The objective was to extend range of the RF-84K Thunderflash nestled in the belly of the B-36 by launching and recovering the aircraft via a large cradle. (*USAF/Richard Ward Collection*)

Next up was the B-36H, which would become the major production variant of this strategic bomber; a total of 156 were built, of which seventy-three were RB-36Hs. These were very similar to the B-36F, but with an improved flight deck which made room for a second flight engineer's station. The 'H' also featured a modern AN/APG-41A radar system, housed inside a pair of tail radomes that guided the 20 mm cannon located in the tail to the target. The first B-36H flew on 5 April 1952 and deliveries started the following December. The RB-36H entered USAF service in 1952 and all were delivered by September 1953. One B-36H was converted as an air refuelling tanker and a single aircraft was converted to carry a nuclear reactor (covered separately).

The final production version of the Peacemaker was the B-36J, which had a pair of extra fuel tanks and a strengthened undercarriage to cope with the additional weight. The fuel capacity was increased by 2,770 gallons, which raised the full capacity to 36,396 gallons and the maximum take-off weight to 410,000 lb. Thirty-three B-36Js were built; the first, designated as the YB-36J, first flew in July 1953, followed by the first production machine in September 1953. Fourteen B-36Js, as were many B-36s before them after production, were built as 'Featherweights', which simply involved the removal of all of the guns except the twin 20 mms in the tail. The crew was reduced and the resulting weight reduction meant that the B-36J could easily operate at a height of 47,000 feet and, in some cases, heights of 50,000 feet could be reached.

The B-36 had a very short service life and some of the earlier machines were being scrapped by early 1956 with the arrival of the Boeing B-52 Stratofortress which, incredibly, is still in service today. With the arrival of the B-52 in numbers, the last Peacemaker to be built, B-36J 52-2827, was retired from duty with the 95th BW at Biggs on 12 February 1959.

B-26H-4-CF 50-1092 'U' of the 11th BW (made up of the 26th, 42nd and 98th BS) operated from Carswell AFB between December 1947 and December 1948. (*USAF/ Richard Ward Collection*)

RB-36H-20-CF 51-13717 with multiple guards in close attendance is an indication as to how sensitive the equipment on board these aircraft was. (*Richard Ward Collection*)

52-2827 was the very last production B-36J-75-CF built and the last operational example of this huge bomber to serve the USAF. Retired from the 95th BW at Biggs AFB, the aircraft was saved from the axe and today is being restored at Pima Air and Space Museum, Tucson, Arizona. (*USAF/ Richard Ward Collection*)

XB/NB-36H 'NEPA'

In the 1940s, the concept of a nuclear-powered aircraft was being taken seriously and the idea that a bomber could remain aloft for days rather than hours was very appealing to the USAAF at the time. A contract was issued to Fairchild, operating at Oak Ridge, Tennessee, in 1946 in order to research the possibility of this latest form of powered flight under the name NEPA (Nuclear Energy for the Propulsion of Aircraft). Not long after, a further study was carried out by the Massachusetts Institute of Technology on behalf of the Atomic Energy Commission which concluded that nuclear power could be used to propel an aircraft, although it would take at least fifteen years to perfect.

However, progress was swift and by 1951 the USAF had decided that the NEPA project had made more than enough progress to begin work on a nuclear power plant. A contract to build the actual unit was awarded to General Electric, which had designed and built a compressor through which air was heated after passing through a reactor and then expelled via a jet pipe. Pratt & Whitney was also tasked with building an indirect cycle engine which employed an intermediate fluid to disperse the heat into the air instead of directing the air over the core of the reactor.

By 1954, the project had advanced to the point of selecting an actual aircraft to test the nuclear power plant, to be given the code name WS-125A. Both Lockheed and Convair were tasked with carrying out the necessary airframe work and the obvious contender at the time for this complex conversion was the B-36 Peacemaker. One particular aircraft, a B-36H, 51-5712, which had been damaged in a tornado at Carswell on 1 September 1952 (one of nineteen B-36s!), did not have a bright future up to this point, but, as the damage was localised to the forward fuselage of the aircraft, this made the B-36 ripe for conversion.

The menacing yet strangely attractive XB-36H, 51-5712, complimented by a long blue and red cheat line down the fuselage, at rest between test flights. (*USAF/Richard Ward Collection*)

It was never the intention to completely convert the donor aircraft to nuclear power and at no point would the B-36 fly using the reactor alone. The aircraft would actually serve as a test bed to measure the effects of radiation on the airframe, general equipment, instruments and to carry out further study into how all systems could be protected from radiation. Mounted in the aft bomb bay, the 1,000 Kw reactor weighed 35,000 lb and was designed to be installed and removed via a crane when on the ground. Numerous apertures were created around the reactor in an effort to keep it cool, while the crew, made up of a pilot, co-pilot, flight engineer and a couple of nuclear engineers, would be protected from the radiation inside a completely re-designed compartment in place of the traditional nose section. The new forward compartment was lined with lead and rubber and further protection was provided by a lead-covered disc mounted in the middle of the fuselage that weighed 4 tons! The windshield was leaded glass a foot thick and was only for the benefit of the pilot and co-pilot while the reactor itself could be observed by the crew via closed-circuit television cameras.

Redesignated the XB-36H and named 'Crusader', the aircraft made its maiden flight on 17 September 1955 in the hands of Arthur S. Witchell Jr. The first of forty-seven test flights began, each of them being carried out over remote areas and at altitude before the reactor was turned on. On each flight, the XB-36H was also accompanied by a Boeing C-97 loaded with Marines who had orders to parachute to

The entire crew of five was contained within a lead and rubber-lined forward compartment and further protection was provided by a modified windshield which was a foot thick! (*USAF/Richard Ward Collection*)

26

Right: One of two nuclear engineers' panels in the cockpit of the XB-36H, and note the good quality image on the TV monitor at the top of the photograph. (*USAF/Richard Ward Collection*)

Below: The 35,000 lb reactor was only turned on at altitude and over a remote area in an effort to reduce risk to people on the ground in the event of an accident. (*USAF/Richard Ward Collection*)

The XB-36H in full colour in company with a Boeing B-50D which was packed with sensitive electronic measuring devices. (*USAF/Richard Ward Collection*)

earth and protect the sensitive aircraft should a crash occur. A heavily instrumented Boeing B-50D also flew with the XB-36H on a number of test flights.

By late 1956, the XB-36H had been redesignated as the NB-36H, but this new title was short-lived as the USAF had already made the decision to shut down the WS-125A project. On 28 March 1957, the NB-36H made its last flight and, before the year was over, was fully decommissioned. In 1958, the aircraft was completely scrapped and all radioactive components were buried deep in the ground in a secret location.

Model 106 Skycoach and Model 111 Aircar

Designed by Stinson, the Model 106 was an experimental four-seat light aircraft with a pusher engine. The latter configuration resulted in a twin-boom arrangement extending from a bulbous cabin with sufficient room for a pilot and three passengers. Power was provided by a 230 hp Franklin engine which drove a cooling fan as well as the propeller. First flight tested from San Diego in April 1946 by Bill Martin, performance was found to be poor, especially compared to the Beechcraft Bonanza, which could cruise at 165 mph, 23 mph faster than the Skycoach's maximum speed, on 65 less horsepower. Only one prototype, registered NX40004, was built and this was scrapped in 1947.

A development of the pre-Second World War Gwinn Aircar, Convair's Model 111 Aircar differed by having a cantilever monoplane wing configuration and a pusher propeller powered by a mid-engine (65 hp Continental C-65) layout. Nicknamed the 'Pregnant Guppy', the Model 111 suffered from innumerable problems ranging from rudder control issues and lack of stability to engine cooling issues. Only one machine was built, with the registration NX90652, and after a number of engines and driveshafts were quickly worn out, the project was discretely dispensed with.

Originally titled 'Skycoach Flight View Reveals Graceful Design And Pleasant Visibility', this is an accurate artist's impression of the Model 106 Skycoach. (*Jack C. Wright/Richard Ward Collection*)

A purposeful-looking machine even at this stage, the Model 106 Skycoach already has its 230 hp Franklin engine installed in this image. (*San Diego Air & Space Museum*)

On paper and in appearance, the Model 106 looked promising but once in the air this twin-boomed four-seater could not match the competition for performance or efficiency. This image was captured on 23 April 1946. (*San Diego Air & Space Museum*)

The Model 111 Aircar nearing completion on 6 May 1946. The mid-mounted engine was accessible and presumably removed from below, as can be seen by the large access panel aft of the starboard mainwheel. (*San Diego Air & Space Museum*)

Adorned with just the registration and the word 'Experimental' on its metal fuselage, the tubby little Model 111 prepares for another test flight. Cooling the 65 hp Continental engine was a major problem but at least one and mostly likely two large air scoops have been installed on the engine panel. (*San Diego Air & Space Museum*)

31

Model 116 and 118 ConVairCar

This concept of a flying car had its roots in the Second World War when designer Theodore P. 'Ted' Hall briefly worked with Consolidated and had the idea of such a machine being used in clandestine-type operations. Post-war, the notion of a flying car never left Ted Hall and, in company with Tommy Thompson, he took the design to the next level. The design appeared in *Popular Mechanics* magazine in 1946 and was labelled as the Convair Model 116.

The Model 116 featured, as its main fuselage/body, a modified Crosley two-seater car which had reasonably aerodynamic lines powered, on the ground, by a 26 hp air-cooled engine. For flight, a monoplane wing was attached to the roof while the tail surfaces were attached to a single boom. In the air, the Model 116 was powered by a 90 hp Franklin air-cooled flat four engine which drove a two-blade wooden propeller. Registered as NX90654, the Model 116 first flew on 12 July 1946 in the hands of Russell Rogers, and this sole prototype made sixty-six successful flights before it was grounded.

Still convinced that there was mileage in the flying car, Hall presented a second machine, officially designated the Model 118 by Convair, unofficially referred to as the ConVairCar and, at one stage, as the Hall Flying Automobile. The Model 118 was considerably more refined than the Model 116 with regard to the car body, which had four seats and was made from plastic to keep the weight down. With the same 25 hp Crosley engine used on the ground, the Model 118 had over twice the power in the air thanks to its Lycoming engine.

Left: The Model 116 was the next stage in Theodore P. 'Ted' Hall's quest to create a flying car for the masses. The Model 116 actually featured a heavily modified Crosley two-seater car for the main body/fuselage. (*San Diego Air & Space Museum*)

Right: With a 90 hp Franklin engine for flight and a 26 hp air-cooled engine for the road, the Model 116 showed promise, but after sixty-six successful flights the machine was grounded for good. (*San Diego Air & Space Museum*)

The Model 118 was clearly more of a wing bolted to a car than a car created to fly. It would certainly have been a more appealing vehicle to drive and Convair was more optimistic about this design than those that had gone before. (*San Diego Air & Space Museum*)

The Model 118, NX90850, in its second form following a serious crash by test pilot Reuben Snodgrass. The Model 118 is pictured in early 1948 with W. G. Griswold at the controls. (*Richard Ward Collection*)

The prototype Model 118, registered as NX90850, made its maiden flight on 15 November 1947 with Reuben Snodgrass at the controls. Just three days later, and following a demonstration flight, the Model 118 ran out of fuel near Lindbergh Field, San Diego, and was wrecked. Snodgrass survived with minor injuries but the Model 118's plastic car body was shattered and the wing was damaged. Allegedly, Snodgrass mistook the full car fuel tank gauge for the aviation fuel gauge, which was very low when he took off.

A second Model 118 was built from the remains of the first and was still registered NX90850. It first flew on 29 January 1948, this time with W. G. Griswold serving as test pilot. Convair had high hopes for the flying car market, boldly predicting that production would reach around the 160,000 mark and that each machine would retail at $1,500. In the end, the idea fizzled out but not before 'Ted' Hall had claimed the rights to the Model 116 and 118 and created his own company, called T. R. Hall Engineering Corp. With the US market awash with reasonably priced light aircraft and an abundance of airfields across the country, the flying car idea was dead in the water.

33

Stinson Model 108

Based on the pre-war Model 105 Voyager, Stinson prepared early for the transition from the wartime production of their L-5 Sentinel to a predicted post-war boom for light civilian aircraft. Similar in configuration to the Model 105, the Model 108 had a longer fuselage in order to make room for four seats. The tail surfaces were revised and improved and at first a 125 hp Lycoming engine was installed. A 150 hp and 165 hp Franklin piston engine would become the preferred power plant for the wide range of Model 108s available.

First flown in 1946, the standard Model 108 featured a cargo door on the starboard side of the fuselage. The first big production example was the Model 108-1, of which 1,507 were built, followed by the Model 108-2 with a 165 hp Franklin 6A4-165-B3, which resulted in a further 1,252 units. The most prolific example was the Model 108-3 Voyager, which had a modified fin and rudder, bigger fuel tanks and a higher gross weight. 1,759 Model 108-3s were built and, by late 1947, a grand total of 5,260 Voyagers had been manufactured. However, the post-war civil aviation boom was destined to be short and, despite the aircraft accounting for half of all four-seat aircraft sold in the US during this period, further interest dropped off quickly. Stinson as a company now found itself in a precarious position and at least 200 aircraft were parked, unsold, outside the factory at Wayne, Michigan. The factory was closed down in July 1948 and, just five months later, Stinson was sold to Piper Aircraft.

Stinson 108-1 Voyager LN-BEK pictured at the Leicester PFA Rally on 5 July 1980. Under Convair's wing, 1,507 108-1s were built out of a total of 5,260 Voyagers; a number of them still survive and fly today. (*Via author*)

Purposeful, sturdy, practical and reliable, the Stinson Model 108 family was one of the more successful post-Second World War civilian designs. (*Richard Ward Collection*)

Model 110

It is incredible how little is known about this pioneering aircraft, which paved the way for one of the world's most successful series of medium-range transport aircraft. However, the short story of the Convair Model 110 is one that has been repeated all over the globe and, to a lesser degree, continues to occur even today. The specification was chosen by a leading airline, who moved the goalposts either during production or after the aircraft was completed. Designed to replace the ubiquitous Douglas DC-3, American Airlines selected the Model 110 instead of the Martin 2-0-2 and worked closely with Convair to develop the aircraft. The Model 110 was a low-wing, twin-engine-powered monoplane with a space for thirty passengers contained within an unpressurised fuselage. Before the aircraft (which was serialled NX90653) first flew, American Airlines had already decided that a thirty-passenger capacity was insufficient and that space for ten more passengers was needed. This decision was not as bad as it sounded and although it was an instant killer for the Model 110, it would lead to the hugely successful CV-240 series, which American Airlines still bought into.

The sole Model 110 made its maiden flight on 8 July 1946 from Lindbergh Field with Art Bussy at the controls and Russell Rogers in the co-pilot's seat. With nothing but the name 'Convair – 110' and its serial on its fuselage, the Model 110 was a good-looking aircraft and this only improved with the CV-240, which retained the wings, a similar power plant and tail configuration but introduced a longer fuselage for increased capacity. Work began on the follow up to the Model 110 as soon as American Airlines changed the criteria and so this very important aircraft only flew for a few hours before it was unceremoniously scrapped.

Left: The prototype Convair 110, NX90653, takes to the air for the first time on 8 July 1946 from Lindbergh Field, San Diego. (*Convair/Richard Ward Collection*)

Right: A good-looking aircraft from any angle, the Convair 110 was the crucial foundation block for a wide range of commercial airliners and military variants, some of which still operate to this day. (*Convair/Richard Ward Collection*)

CV-240 Family Including the CV-240, 340, 440, C-131 Samaritan, T-29 and R4Y

Later known as the Convairliner, the Convair CV-240 (NX90849) made its maiden flight on 16 March 1947. There was no need for a prototype, the Model 110 serving in that role as the new CV-240 retained the same configuration but introduced a longer fuselage which made the rather tubby-looking Model 110 look much sleeker. With just a 3 foot 8 inch extension, passenger capacity was raised to forty, which rendered the CV-240 considerably more appealing not only to the main purchasing airline, American Airlines, but also a number of others waiting in the wings. The CV-240 first entered service with American Airlines on 1 June 1948, launching into a market which was incredibly competitive. Replacing the DC-3 completely was an impossible task because the market was flooded with them and would remain this way for decades, although the CV-240 would fare better than its direct competitor, the Martin 4-0-4, and when production ended, 571 had been built although 395 of these were military variants.

The prototype Convair CV-240, NX90848, over San Diego in 1947. The aircraft enjoyed a long career, which included being converted to Allison T38 engines to become a CV-240-21. In this configuration the aircraft first flew on 29 December 1950, becoming the first turboprop-powered flight in the USA. Remarkably, this aircraft remained on the civil register until January 2003. (*Richard Ward Collection*)

Left: The functional 'office' of the prototype Convair CV-240, NX90848, in around 1947. (*Richard Ward Collection*)

Right: These Pan American stewardesses appear to be quite happy with their brand-new CV-240, NC90659 *Clipper Bahamas*, later renamed *Clipper Cuba*, in around 1948. (*Richard Ward Collection*)

The first of several military variants was the T-29A which, as the XAT-29, first flew on 22 September 1949. The USAF needed a 'flying classroom' type aircraft in which it could train navigators and radar operators. Based completely on the CV-240, the T-29A (forty-six built) differed only in not being pressurised and externally featuring four astrodomes along the spine for student navigators. The T-29B (105 built) featured a pressurised fuselage with space for ten navigators and four radar operators while the T-29C (119 built) was installed with more powerful engines. The final variant, the T-29D (ninety-three built), was produced as an advanced bombing/navigation trainer with space for six students and was equipped with a 'K' system bombsight and recording equipment for bombing results. There were also a number of 'spin-off' variants such as the military VIP VT-29A/B/C and D and the AT-29/ET-29C and D for checking airways navigational aids and, like all T-29s, this hard-working aircraft served the USAF and US Navy.

In the meantime, Convair was working hard to develop the already promising CV-240 and this resulted in the CV-340, which was first flown by Ellis D. 'Sam' Shannon and Phil Prophett. Work began in 1951 and the key improvements were more powerful R-2800-CB16/17 engines and a further stretch of the fuselage by 4 feet 6 inches, which allowed the aircraft a capacity of forty-four passengers. To cope with the higher gross weight, the wing area was also increased by over 100 sq. ft. These subtle but significant changes finally moved the Convair airliner into a DC-3 beater and the loyal United Airlines finally replaced its Douglas machines with the CV-340, which first entered service with United on 28 March 1952.

The last of the radial piston-engined variants was the CV-440 which, on the outside at least, looked little different from the CV-340 and was, in fact, a conversion of the latter rather than a 'new build'. Also known as the CV-440 Metropolitan, the aircraft had much-improved sound proofing and the option for

Convair T-29A 49-1936 '203/TP-936' was one of forty-six 'flying classrooms' for the USAF, many which were still serving in the 1970s. (*San Diego Air & Space Museum*)

T-29B (ex-T-29A) 0-91941 of the Base Flight taxies for take-off from its home station at RAF Sculthorpe in Norfolk. (*Richard Ward Collection*)

119 T-29Cs were built with more powerful engines than the 'A' and 'B', including this aircraft, 53-3475 '429/TP-475'. Later converted to a VIP VT-29C, this aircraft was sent to MASDC on 20 December 1974 and was broken up on 27 October 1977. (*San Diego Air & Space Museum*)

VIP VT-29B 0-15125 of the Air Force Communication Service. (*Candid Aero-Files, R. W. Harrison*)

The prototype CV340 'Convair-Liner', N3401, which featured a longer fuselage, giving the aircraft a passenger capacity of forty-four. After serving Convair for many years as a test bed, this machine was sold to Spain, was re-registered as EC-BBV and continued to serve with the Spanish Air Force until the late 1970s. (*Richard Ward Collection*)

The starboard Pratt & Whitney R-2800-97 engine of CV-340-35 NX90853 receives some attention before delivery to Continental Air Lines in early 1953. The aircraft had a very short career as it was written off at Midland Airport, Texas, on 16 March 1954 when it crashed after take-off. (*Richard Ward Collection*)

Delivered as a CV-340-48 in May 1954, KLM's PH-CGB *Jan Van Scorel* was later converted to CV-440-4 standard. The aircraft went on to serve with ALM Antillean Airlines and had a spell in Panama before joining American Jet Industries in 1974. Another long-server, the aircraft was not cancelled from the register until 2012. (*Richard Ward Collection*)

Left: As clean as a whistle, this CV-440 is giving nothing away with regard to its true identity. This successful airliner had matured into an attractive domestic workhorse. (*Convair/Richard Ward Collection*)

Right: SAS (Scandinavian Airline System) CV-440-75 SE-BSP *Rollo Viking* taxies to a halt at London Heathrow Airport in the early 1960s. The aircraft ended its days as a police trainer at Stockholm Airport before being broken up in 1978. (*Richard Ward Collection*)

Converted back in 1953 from a CV-340-68A to a CV-440, this aircraft served a number of companies before being chartered by Alice Cooper in the mid-1970s. The aircraft was christened *Margherita*. (*Richard Ward Collection*)

a higher density seating arrangement which could raise passenger capacity from forty-four to fifty-two. All CV-440s were converted CV-340s and, in all, 155 were altered to the new standard. First flown on 6 October 1955, this was a popular conversion for many airlines.

The next military variant and the first transport version for the USAF was the C-131A Samaritan (twenty-six built). Specifically designed for casualty evacuation duties, the C-131A was based on the CV-240 but was modified to include big cargo doors for stretchers or bulky cargo. There was enough room for twenty-seven stretcher cases or thirty-seven seated casualties. The C-131B (thirty-six built) was designed for transport and/or electronic test work and was followed by the C-131D (twenty-seven built), which was effectively a military version of the CV-340, and the VC-131D (six built) VIP/Staff transport, a military CV-440. The ECM C-131E (fifteen built and a single conversion from a C-131D), later TC-131E, was next. All of them were delivered during 1956 and 1957. A photographic survey variant was designated the RC-131F (six conversions), not to mention an array of other conversions which included the JC-131B (nine conversions) for missile tracking; the EC-131G (one conversion) as an electronics trainer; the RC-131G (one conversion) for airways navigation aids; and the odd-looking NC-131H (one conversion), N21466, which had a second cockpit section installed to the nose for in-flight simulator duties.

The first 'vomit comets' used by NASA for their Reduced Gravity Program were three C-131A Samaritans, including this machine, NASA-707. (*Richard Ward Collection*)

A rare image of 3rd Air Force (RAF Northolt) C-131D 55-291 on static at RAF Wethersfield in May 1959. Sadly, this machine hit the headlines for all the wrong reasons when it crashed taking off from Münich-Riem Airport on 17 December 1960. All twenty onboard and thirty-two on the ground were killed. (*Richard Ward Collection*)

A missile-tracking JC-131B, 53-6699 of the Air Research Development Command, in around 1960. Nine aircraft, 53-7788, 7791, 7795, 7796, 7799, 7804, 7806, 7810 and 7822, were converted from a standard C-131B to this configuration. (*Richard Ward Collection*)

R4Y-1 (later re-designated as the C-131F) 141017 '017/RP' in US Navy service with VR-1. (*Richard Ward Collection*)

No. 412 (Transport) Squadron, CAF, CC-109 Cosmopolitan 109159. (*Richard Ward Collection*)

The US Navy also operated a number of C-131s although these were all redesignated as the R4Y. Most prolific was the CV-440-based R4Y-1 (thirty-six built), later redesignated as the C-131F, which served as a general transport, personnel transport and evacuation transport. A 'one off' machine was the R4Y-1Z, which served as a US Navy staff transport and was later redesignated as VC-131F. A pair of C-131Es was transferred to the US Navy to become R4Y-2s, which were later known as C-131Gs and served in the transport role. The US Navy also operated a few T-29Bs that were inherited from the USAF and continued to operate the type well into the 1980s.

The RCAF (later the CAF) also operated a CV-440 derivative in the shape of the CC-109 Cosmopolitan. These good looking machines were powered by a pair of Napier Eland turboprops, a conversion that was carried out by Canadair. Serving solely with No. 412 (Transport) Squadron out of Ottawa, these reliable aircraft were operated between 1960 and 1994 in the VIP role.

CV-540 Family
Including the CV-540, 580, 600, 640 and 5800

As touched upon in the CV-240 family story, thanks to the arrival of the turboprop a great number of aircraft were converted to this new, more powerful, form of propulsion. The CV-240 family was no exception and due to its robust structure and functional design it was most suited to turboprop power. The first of many conversions took place in 1954 when Napier & Sons in Britain installed a pair of 3,060 ehp Eland NEI.1 turboprops in a CV-240. This aircraft first flew on 9 February 1955 and the type, redesignated the CV-540, first entered service with Allegheny Airlines not long after. Only five were converted and when development of the Eland turboprop ended in 1962, these aircraft were reconverted back to piston power.

PacAero Engineering Corporation, based in Santa Monica, began to convert CV-340s and CV-440s by installing a pair of 3,750 ehp Allison 501-D13 turboprops. To cope with the greater power, the fin, rudder and elevators were enlarged. Designated the CV-580, but also known as the 'Super Convair', these machines could carry fifty-two passengers, the first of them taking to the air on 19 January 1960. However, the CV-580 did not enter service until June 1964, with Frontier Airlines.

One of two CV-540s leased from Canadair for Quebecair was this aircraft, CF-LMN. Attractive-looking aircraft that were popular with crews, these Quebecair machines were silver on the underside of the fuselage, broken up by a large black-banded cheatline with white uppersides. (*Richard Ward Collection*)

Another rare image is this CV-580, N73121, in service with Gem State Airlines for a period that only lasted a few weeks between December 1979 and January 1980. (*Richard Ward Collection*)

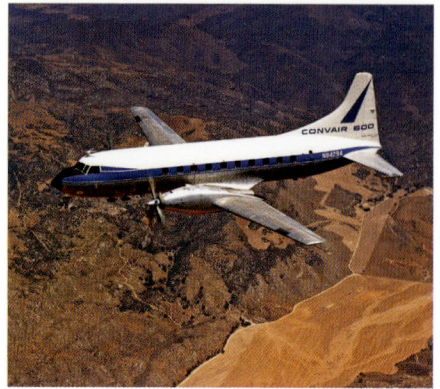

Left: Still in Columbian Air Force service is this CV-580, EJC-121, which began its life as a standard CV-230 back in 1953 with Braniff International. (*Richard Ward Collection*)

Right: The Convair turboprop version of the CV-240 was originally designated as the CV-240D and then again as the CV-600, as presented here with N94294 on 18 August 1965. In the latter form, this aircraft was delivered to Central Airlines in December 1965 with the new serial N74859. (*San Diego Air & Space Museum*)

Norcanair CV-640 C-GQCQ which, after further service with Canada West Air, was delivered to the Hamilton Aviation Museum, Tucson, in early 1996. (*Richard Ward Collection*)

Convair joined the turboprop conversion bandwagon by offering a wide range of aircraft. They were all powered by a pair of 3,025 ehp Rolls-Royce RDa.10/1 Dart turboprops, which could be installed in the CV-240, 340 or 440. The CV-240 was the only one of the three which was given additional airframe strength and this was made even more appealing by raising the passenger capacity to forty-eight compared to the CV-340 and 440, which were now offered as fifty-six-seaters. Initially redesignated by Convair as the CV-240D, 340D and 440D, these designations were later changed to the CV-600 for the CV-240D while the CV-340D and 440D were collectively re-named as the CV-640. The first CV-600 turboprop entered service with Central Airlines on 30 November 1965 and was followed by the first CV-640, which joined Caribair on 22 December 1965.

Also worthy of mention is the CV-5800, which was a conversions of ex-US Navy C-131Fs by Kelowna Flightcraft Ltd, based in Canada. Not just a turboprop conversion, the CV-5800 also involved stretching the fuselage by 16 feet 7 inches and adding a new freight door and a full digital avionics suite in the cockpit, including EFIS, all of which was powered by a pair of Allison 501-D22G engines. First flown on 11 February 1992, only six of these impressive machines were converted; all of them, at one point or another, served with Contract Air Cargo.

XB-46

By early 1944, the USAAF was becoming anxious that the Germans had made great advances in the development of jet-powered bombers. The War Department responded by issuing a remit for a new generation of jet bombers with weights ranging from 80,000 to 200,000 lb, a maximum speed of 500 mph, a 40,000 foot ceiling and a range of at least 1,000 miles. This specification was presented to the nation's aircraft manufacturers in April 1944 and on 6 November Convair presented its proposal. While superbly aerodynamic, the Convair design remained conventional with its shoulder-mounted wing mounted to a very streamlined and attractive fuselage. The slender Davis wing had near full-span Fowler flaps along its trailing edge while roll control was achieved with spoilers that were 20 feet long, compared to the traditional ailerons which were a mere 6 feet long. Power would be provided by four General Electric TG-180 axial-flow turbojets which were mounted in a pair of equally streamlined underwing pods that concealed the main pneumatic undercarriage when retracted. The three-man crew was accommodated in the forward fuselage. The pilot and co-pilot were in tandem, in a near fighter-type configuration, while the bombardier sat inside a glazed nose.

Right: The sole XB-46, 45-59582, takes shape at Convair's San Diego plant in late 1946 or early 1947. Note the part-built XC-99 in the background. (*San Diego Air & Space Museum*)

Below: A good view of the XB-46's 20-foot-long spoilers in place of traditional ailerons for roll control. (*Convair/Richard Ward Collection*)

Yet another good-looking design, the slender 106-foot-long fuselage of the XB-46 gave this jet bomber an elegant appearance. Just four months after the XB-46 first flew, the programme was shut down. (*Richard Ward Collection*)

The XB-46 was taken on strength by the USAF on 7 November 1947; now fitted with J35 turbojets, the aircraft continued flight testing from West Palm Beach AFB until a lack of spares forced an indefinite grounding. (*USAF/Richard Ward Collection*)

Convair referred to this new jet bomber as the Model 109 and, when an order came in for three prototypes, the machine was designated as the XB-46 and serialled 45-59582 to 45-59584. This would be a tough production order to win as prototypes were also ordered from North American (XB-45), Boeing (XB-47) and Martin (XB-48). As the end of the war approached and large orders and new designs for military aircraft started to be cancelled, this group of prototypes escaped the axe, mainly because the USAAF would need a new generation of bombers during peacetime. However, the Convair order was reduced to a single aircraft, which at least meant that funds could be re-directed to other projects.

By 1946, the USAAF was feeling the pressure to get a new jet bomber into service as soon as possible but at that stage only the XB-45 and XB-46 were close to completion while the XB-47 and XB-48 would not be ready for a further two years. As a result, the XB-45 and XB-46 were tested first; one of them would be selected for production while the XB-47 or XB-48 would be chosen as well if they turned out to be superior to the early selection. The North American XB-45 Tornado was a very conventional aircraft which pushed no boundaries, unlike the XB-46, which looked amazing but from an operational point of view was impractical, and that was just with regard to the internal equipment. On 2 August 1945, the XB-45 was selected for production.

XB-46 45-59582 made its maiden flight on 2 April 1947 with 'Sam' Shannon and Bill Martin at the controls. In August 1947, the XB-46 programme was closed down and, by the following month, the last of fourteen company test flights had been completed at Muroc. The XB-46 was then re-fitted with a set of Allison J35-A-3 turbojets and delivered to Wright Field, where it was taken on strength by the USAF on 7 November 1947. The aircraft then took part in a number of flight tests from West Palm Beach AFB from August 1948 to August 1949, by which time, as would befit a single prototype, serviceability became a problem due to a distinct lack of spare components. However, the XB-46 soldiered on and in July 1950 was performing low temperature tests at Eglin Field to record the effect on the bomber's pneumatic systems, which not only powered the undercarriage but also the brakes, bomb bay doors and crew doors. When this task was complete, the USAF had no further use for the XB-46, which was broken up in early 1952, but at least the nose section survived and was sent to Wright-Patterson for preservation.

XC-99

The largest piston-engined land-based transport aircraft in the world when it first flew in 1947, the colossal XC-99 was developed from the B-36. The aircraft retained the B-36's engines, wings and tail unit, while the long cylindrical body was replaced by a two-deck fuselage of huge capacity. The aircraft was designed to carry a payload of 100,000 lb but, once operational, this would be breached by at least 4,000 lb. There was room for 400 soldiers and their equipment or 300 stretcher cases; there was even a cargo lift installed on board. While Convair intended the XC-99 as a military transport aircraft, the company also proposed a civilian variant known as the Model 37. Capable of carrying over 200 passengers a distance of 4,200 miles, there was some interest from civil airlines, including Pan Am, who placed an order for fifteen aircraft. While the military gave little priority to the cost of actually operating aircraft like this, the Wasp Major radials were far too thirsty for the civilian market and, sadly, the project was abandoned before a suitably economical unit had been developed.

The prototype XC-99, serialled 45-52436, made its maiden flight on 24 November 1947 and was in service with the USAF from 26 May 1949 until 19 March 1957. At first the aircraft was fitted with large, single-wheel main undercarriage units, which were replaced by bogies before it served with the USAF, and it also gained a weather radar unit. The sole example of the XC-99 had an amazing career, during which it racked up more than 7,400 flying hours and transported over 27,000 tons of cargo across the globe. The aircraft was something of a 'celebrity' and wherever it went there was always a crowd to greet it.

The XC-99 made its final flight into Kelly AFB, a place where it was destined to remain for a further forty-seven years. The aircraft was dismantled in 2004 and moved, piece by piece, to Wright-Patterson and then again to Davis-Monthan, where it sits today pending a full and potentially costly restoration.

The majestic sight of the world's largest piston-engined, land-based transport aircraft, which first flew on 24 November 1957. (*USAF/Richard Ward Collection*)

Above: The sole XC-99, 45-52436, dwarfs the second production Convair CV-240 Convair-Liner, NX90849. (*Convair/Richard Ward Collection*)

Below: The giant XC-99 during its twilight period of USAF service in MATS trim and a ten-year-old '0' prefix to its serial number. This impressive aircraft was retired on 19 March 1957 and flown to Kelly AFB, where it was destined to remain for forty-seven years. (*USAF/Richard Ward Collection*)

XF-92

At the very end of the Second World War, the USAAF had already set its sights on a new supersonic fighter. The gauntlet was dropped and an ambitious criteria for this new aircraft was announced in August 1945: a capability to reach 50,000 ft in 4 minutes and a maximum speed of 700 mph.

Convair immediately stepped up to the plate and its ramjet-powered fighter with a wing sweep of 45 degrees won the contract in May 1946. Initially designated the XP-92, the design encountered problems early on when wind tunnel tests exposed potential lateral control problems and wing tip stalling issues at low angles of attack. Falling back on research carried out by Dr Alexander Lippisch for the Germans during the war, Convair made the wise decision to make the XP-92 a delta. The first of many power plants for this ground-breaking aircraft was a 1,560 lb Westinghouse J30-WE-1 turbojet backed up by six 2,000 lb rocket engines! There was no doubt that the XP-92 was designed for nothing more than to intercept the target as quickly as possible and no thought was given to endurance with such a configuration.

By November 1946, the USAAF was already getting impatient and to speed things up they authorised Convair to build a delta-winged research prototype. This aircraft was given the company designation of the Model 7-002 and the military serial 46-682, the first of three such potential machines, although 46-683 and 46-684 were never built. With pressure building and the prospect of the project having the plug pulled on it at any moment, Convair worked flat out to create the XP-92, which had as many 'home grown' components as possible. As such, the power plant and hydraulics system were from a Lockheed P-80 Shooting Star, the main undercarriage was poached from a North American FJ-1 Fury while the nose wheel leg was from a Bell P-63 Kingcobra; even the rudder pedals, the most vintage components, were lifted from a Vultee BT-13 Valiant! The delta configuration meant that the aircraft had no traditional tailplane with elevators, just a single fin and rudder; lateral and pitch control was therefore achieved through elevons (elevators and ailerons combined) which, like all of the machine's flight controls, were hydraulically controlled.

Convair XF-92A 46-682 on the Muroc Dry Lake in 1948. (*USAF/ Richard Ward Collection*)

'Sam' Shannon sits in the cockpit of the XF-92A, which first flew from Muroc on 18 September 1948. (*USAF/Richard Ward Collection*)

The XF-92 in all-white gloss finish with the exception of a black non-reflective area in front of the cockpit, grey flight surfaces and bright red painted inside the air intake. (*Richard Ward Collection*)

Convair XF-92A (Model 7-002) 46-682 in good company with a band of 'X-Planes' at Edwards AFB. (*USAF/Richard Ward Collection*)

The XF-92A did not enjoy an easy flight test career; both its Allison J33-A-29 and later J33-A16 engines failed to provide the thrust to push the aircraft through the sound barrier. Regardless, the amount of data gathered by Convair would lead to the successful F-102 and later the F-106. (*Richard Ward Collection*)

Released in 1957, the film *Jet Pilot* starring John Wayne and Janet Leigh also featured a large number of interesting aircraft dating back to the early 1950s. One of them was the XF-92A, masquerading as a Russian fighter complete with 'discreet' 'MIG 23' markings on the tail. (*USAF/Richard Ward Collection*)

Work was progressing well up to the summer of 1947 when some disruption was caused by Vultee Field closing. The XP-92 was then transported to San Diego and, by the autumn of 1947, was complete. In December of that year, the airframe was taken to Moffett Field for wind tunnel testing at NACA's Ames Aeronautical Laboratory.

After returning to San Diego, the XP-92's first serious power plant, in the shape of a 4,250 lb Allison J33-A-21 turbojet, was installed. Once again, the aircraft hit the road and in April 1948 was ready for taxiing and high speed ground run trials at Muroc Dry Lake, which would later evolve into Edwards AFB. On 9 June 1948, the aircraft, which was redesignated as the XF-92A, made a very small hop into the air and all early signs were good. Not long after, and as predicted, the USAF decided that the whole concept was not a great idea, although the possibilities of a delta-winged fighter had not been lost on them and work continued on the XF-92A.

Prior to flight testing proper, the XF-92A was installed with a 5,200 lb Allison J33-A-23 turbojet and on 18 September 1948 the aircraft made its maiden flight from Muroc in the hands of 'Sam' Shannon, becoming the world's first delta-winged aircraft to take to the air. Flight testing continued apace between Shannon and Bill Martin. On 26 August 1949, preliminary flight testing was completed and the XF-92A was signed over to the USAF. Military trials continued in the hands of Major Frank K. 'Pete' Everest and Captain Charles E. 'Chuck' Yeager, the former carrying out the bulk of the work. Preliminary flight testing had exposed the fact that the flight controls were extremely sensitive while the military test pilots had found the aircraft very easy to land and very stable at speeds approaching the sound barrier. The latter was never broken in level flight, although this was achieved at least once by Major Everest in a dive.

The B-36 was always useful for providing scale during the 1950s and this image with the XF-92A is no exception. The B-36 was 162 feet 1 inch long while the diminutive (by comparison) XF-92A was a mere 42 feet 6 inches long! Only a short period separated their maiden flights but their technology was poles apart. (*USAF/ Richard Ward Collection*)

The problem of performance was deemed to be a lack of power; therefore, in 1951 the XP-92A was fitted with a 7,500 lb Allison J33-A29 turbojet. Convair had high hopes that this would easily push the XP-92A through the sound barrier and, on 20 July 1951, Captain Yeager took the re-engined delta back into the air. Disappointingly, there was very little improvement in the overall performance and the J33-A-29 proved to be a troublesome unit; as a result, only twenty-one flights were made over a nineteen-month period. A final engine change was called for, this time to an 8,400 lb Allison J33-A16 which was flight tested for the first time by Albert Scott Crossfield on 9 April 1953. Operating the aircraft on behalf of NACA, Crossfield found that the XP-92A had the disturbing habit of pitching up during high-speed turns and, as a result, wing fences were installed which only partly cured the problem. The XF-92A programme came to an undignified end on 14 October 1953 when the nose wheel collapsed during a high-speed taxi run and the damaged suffered was deemed beyond economical repair.

The XF-92A was a pioneering aircraft and the information gleaned from its delta wing alone paved the way for the highly successful F-102 and F-106 interceptors, which provided the backbone of US national aerial defence into the early 1980s. As for 46-682, the aircraft was left to the elements on static display but was thankfully rescued by the USAF in 1962 and moved to Wright-Patterson, where it remains to this day.

R3Y Tradewind

In 1945, the US Navy began to make public their potential requirement for a long-range, multi-role flying boat. Capitalising on technology gained during the Second World War, this new flying boat would incorporate a laminar flow wing and a turboprop engine which was still in the early stages of development. The latter, significant component would seal the fate of this project from the outset.

Convair's design proposal was accepted by the US Navy and on 27 May 1946 a contract was awarded for two prototype aircraft. Under the designation XP5Y-1 (Model 3), this flying boat was big; the single-step fuselage would be nearly 140 feet long but would only have a length-to-beam ratio of 10 to 1, which also made it very slender and aerodynamic. The large 145-foot span wing would have a quartet of turboprops, provided by Allison, in the shape of the T40-A-4 turboprop, each of which was fitted with a pair of six-blade contra-rotating propellers driven through a common gearbox. Part of the 'multi-role' remit for this aircraft was for it to carry very advanced radar equipment, ECM and MAD, plus a substantial load of weapons (up to 8,000 lb), ranging from bombs and mines to rockets and torpedoes. Provision for a defensive armament suite of five pairs of 20 mm cannon, located in the nose, tail and rear fuselage beam positions, was also incorporated into the design.

The prototype, serialled 121455, carried out its maiden flight on 18 April 1950 and immediately entered the record books by becoming the world's first turboprop-powered flying boat. A further record was added in August when the XP5Y-1 established a new turboprop endurance record of 8 hours 6 minutes. At this stage, everything looked rosy for this impressive aircraft. However, out of the blue,

The prototype XP5Y-1, 121455 takes to the air for the first time on 18 April 1950, instantly becoming the world's first turboprop-powered flying boat. (*Convair/Richard Ward Collection*)

An R3Y-1 Tradewind captured not far from NAS Miramar in 1956. (*Convair/Richard Ward Collection*)

A Convair R3Y-1 of VR-2 at rest at NAS Alameda, California. The large 'bulge' on the side of the forward fuselage, and on the rear fuselage as well, was the cannon position, which as you can see in this view is devoid of armament. (*Convair/ Richard Ward Collection*)

the US Navy suddenly decided that it had no need for a long-range patrol flying boat and instead requested that Convair re-design the aircraft to carry passengers and freight/cargo instead.

It was not exactly a 'back to the drawing board' moment but it would take time to redesign an aircraft of this magnitude. In the meantime, Convair continued to flight test 121455 while work carried on with the second prototype, serialled 121456. This flight test programme came to an abrupt halt on 15 July 1953 when XP5Y-1 121455 crashed into the sea 6 miles off Point Loma, California, because of what was believed to have been a multiple engine failure. Luckily, all eleven crew onboard managed to bail out and survived.

Work continued on the passenger and cargo-carrying variant, which was designated the R3Y-1 and named 'Tradewind'. Design changes included a new tailplane without a dihedral and a cargo hatch; this was 10 feet wide and installed aft of the wing on the port side of the rear fuselage. The engine nacelles were also redesigned to accommodate the supposedly improved Allison T40-A-10 turboprops. On top of that, the fuselage was made considerably more comfortable, complete with air conditioning, sound-proofing and pressurisation for up to 103 passengers or ninety-two stretchers plus a dozen attendants. The R3Y-1 had an impressive cargo payload of 24 tons. The first aircraft, which was effectively the first production machine, was serialled 128445 and made its maiden flight on 25 February 1954. Further records would tumble, beginning on 24 February 1955 when one aircraft flew from the west coast of the US to the east at an average speed of 403 mph. Another machine flew non-stop from Honolulu to Alameda on 18 October 1955 in 6 hours and 45 minutes at an average speed of 360 mph. Only five R3Y-1s (128445 to 128449) were built but, just like the prototype, these

An R3Y-2 demonstrates some if its load-carrying capability as approximately eighty soldiers disembark. (*Richard Ward Collection*)

The hinged nose of the R3Y-2 was a novel feature which created an aperture 8 feet 4 inches wide and 6 feet 8 inches high. This feature is being demonstrated here on an incomplete airframe; note the lack of propellers and possibly engine on the port wing. (*Richard Ward Collection*)

aircraft certainly made a big impression. After initial trials at the NATC at Patuxent River, Maryland, the five R3Y-1s were assigned to VR-2 at NAS Alameda, California, from 31 March 1956. All of them were given names pertinent to one of the world's oceans, such as 128446 which was christened *Indian Ocean Tradewind*.

The exact details of the Tradewind's production contract are not fully clear but it is known that, after the R3Y-1, only a further six aircraft were built under the designation R3Y-2. This variant differed considerably from the R3Y-1 thanks to its role as an assault transport aircraft complete with a large upward opening door at the front. The aperture created at the front of the aircraft measured 8 feet 4 inches wide and 6 feet 8 inches high and, thanks to a built-in loading ramp, vehicles and men could be delivered directly onto a beach. Because of the redesigned nose, the cockpit was repositioned much higher than the R3Y-1s. The first R3Y-2, 128450, which was originally ordered as an R3Y-1, made its maiden flight on 22 December 1954. On paper the concept looked great but in practice it was incredibly difficult for the pilot to hold the aircraft steady during loading and unloading. Despite these practical problems, all six of the production R3Y-2s were assigned to VR-2; however, two of them were placed straight into storage at Alameda. One R3Y-2, 131723, was converted into a four-point aerial tanker and, in September 1956, again contributed to the record books by refuelling four F9F-8 Cougars at the same time.

Of the eleven production aircraft, VR-2 were now operating nine, but the unreliable T40 engines were proving to be a headache for the engineers. The contra-rotating propellers and complex gearbox also proved to be troublesome, and on 10 May 1957 the first of two propeller separations took place.

R3Y-2 128450 was originally ordered as an R3Y-1 and with the name *South Atlantic Tradewind* served, like all of these flying boats, with VR-2 at NAS Alameda. (*Convair/Richard Ward Collection*)

The Tradewind entered the records again when R3Y-2 131723 was converted into a four-point tanker capable of refuelling a quartet of F9F-8 Cougars. (*US Navy/Richard Ward Collection*)

A second, more public, incident took place at Alameda after R3Y-1 128446 *Indian Ocean Tradewind* lost a propeller while flying from Keehi Lagoon, Hawaii, to Alameda on 24 January 1958. The pilot was convinced that the departing propeller had damaged the aircraft's hull and, as such, decided to put the aircraft down in the more shallow carrier lagoon close to the flying boat station. When he touched down, the pilot selected reverse thrust but, unknowingly, he had no control of that engine and, with the unit jammed in reverse, the flying boat swung into a sea wall, fortunately without injury to his crew. This was enough to convince the US Navy that the Tradewind's days were numbered and, on 16 April 1958, VR-2 was disbanded. This was a potentially great aircraft that was sadly let down by having the wrong engines.

YB-60

Despite the fact that Boeing had a significant head start with regard to providing the USAF with its first jet-powered long-range strategic bomber, Convair still chanced its arm by proposing an all-jet version of the B-36. Convair issued a proposal to the USAF on 25 August 1950 for a swept-wing version of the B-36 powered by eight Pratt & Whitney J57-P-3 turbojets, which would also power the forthcoming B-52 Superfortress. Not distracted by its commitment to Boeing, the USAF placed an order for a pair of aircraft which were initially to be designated the YB-36G. The two machines were conversions of B-36Fs, 49-2676 and 49-2684, and before either was completed, it was apparent that these swept-winged, jet-powered machines were so different from the original B-36 that they were redesignated the YB-60.

Considerably cheaper to build than a B-52, thanks to 72 per cent of the parts being common to the original B-36, the YB-60's main differences were its 37 degree swept wing and tail surfaces, the under-wing pod-mounted J57 engines, which were neatly installed in four pairs, and a drogue parachute for landing. These differences aside, the swept wing still used a large number of B-36 components

The only YB-60 to fly was 49-2676, which began life on the production line as a B-36F. (*Richard Ward Collection*)

The YB-60, seen on the Fort Worth line, presents a good view of the bomber's swept wing and podded Pratt & Whitney J57-P-3 turbojets. (*USAF/Richard Ward Collection*)

The YB-60's 37 degree main wing sweep is clearly evident in this image of 49-2676. The YB-60 certainly looked the part but it lacked the performance figures of the Boeing B-52, which the USAF had already set its heart upon. (*USAF/Richard Ward Collection*)

which, again, reduced costs and shortened the build and development time. With the latter in mind, the first aircraft (and the only YB-60 destined to fly), 49-2676, flew for the first time on 18 April 1952 with Beryl Erickson in the Captain's seat, only three days after the YB-52 also made its maiden flight.

On paper the YB-60 looked like a promising contender but it was 100 mph slower than the YB-52 and did not handle as well. The YB-60 could potentially carry a bomb load of 72,000 lb compared to the YB-52's 43,000 lb but the USAF had already made up its mind and the Convair machine was cancelled on 20 January 1953. Both aircraft were scrapped in July 1954.

F-102 Delta Dagger

As mentioned earlier, the XF-92A was instrumental to the development of one of Convair's biggest successes with regard to fighter aircraft, in the shape of the F-102 (Model 8) Delta Dagger. Long before Convair was contracted to build the XF-92A, the USAF had been keen to possess a fighter capable of intercepting Soviet intercontinental bombers and this project was formulated under an Advanced Development Objective (ADO). This particular ADO stood out above the rest simply because it called for a complete 'weapons system' rather than following the usual route of acquiring an airframe and then attaching the weapons to it. This time, a new aircraft would be created from multiple systems which would be integrated into the completed machine.

Originally known as Project MX-1554, requests for ideas for a new interceptor from multiple manufacturers was distributed on 18 June 1950. In October 1950, the Hughes Aircraft Company won a contract for the development of Project MX-1179 Electronic Control System which was specifically designed for the interceptor's fire control system and was supposed to be fully compatible with the MX-1554 airframe. Unfortunately, MX-1179 failed to deliver in the required time frame and was abandoned in favour of the Hughes E-9 (later MG-3), which would later be replaced by the MG-10 system.

In January 1951, six manufacturers had put forward their proposals for the MX-1554 but only Convair, Lockheed and Republic were selected to build mock-ups of their designs. However, it was apparent from an early stage that this project had the potential to be a very expensive exercise and the USAF wisely decided to selected one manufacturer who would proceed to the prototype stage. On 11 September 1951 Convair was awarded the contract to build a prototype interceptor powered by a Westinghouse J40 turbojet pending the arrival of the more powerful Wright J67. On 24 November 1951, a decision was made to begin production of the Model 8-80, which would simply be labelled as an 'interim project' rather than the final fully integrated 'weapons system' that the USAF actually wanted.

Ten YF-102s were ordered; the first of them, 52-7994, was flown by test pilot Richard L. Johnson out of Edwards for the first time on 24 October 1953. Early performance figures for the YF-102 were not encouraging. It was partly let down by an under-performing J40 engine which failed completely in November, resulting in a forced landing and a wrecked aircraft; Johnson escaped without injury. The second YF-102, 52-7995, fared no better performance-wise and, at this point, the whole programme was in jeopardy as the aircraft was performing little better than a North American F-86D Sabre!

Now was the time for a partial return to the drawing board for the Convair fighter, a redesign which would incorporate an area-ruled fuselage created from results gathered by NACA scientist Richard Whitcomb. The result was a new wasp or coke bottle-shaped fuselage which was created, in part, by lengthening it by 11 feet. Now redesignated as the YF-102A (Model 8-90), the first of four such machines was rolled out just 117 days after the redesign began and, given serial number 53-1787, made its maiden flight at Edwards on 2 December 1954. Now powered by a Pratt & Whitney J57 turbojet, the YF-102 reached Mach 1.22 and an altitude of 53,000 feet during its first flight!

On 1 May 1956, the first of nearly 1,000 F-102A Delta Daggers was delivered to the 327th FIS, ADC at George AFB. By late 1958, twenty-six ADC squadrons were re-equipped with the F-102A, which had only been named the Delta Dagger the previous year. 627 F-102As would go on to serve with the ADC and, at its peak, thirty-two ADC units would fly the type, although a few did venture beyond the boundaries of the USA.

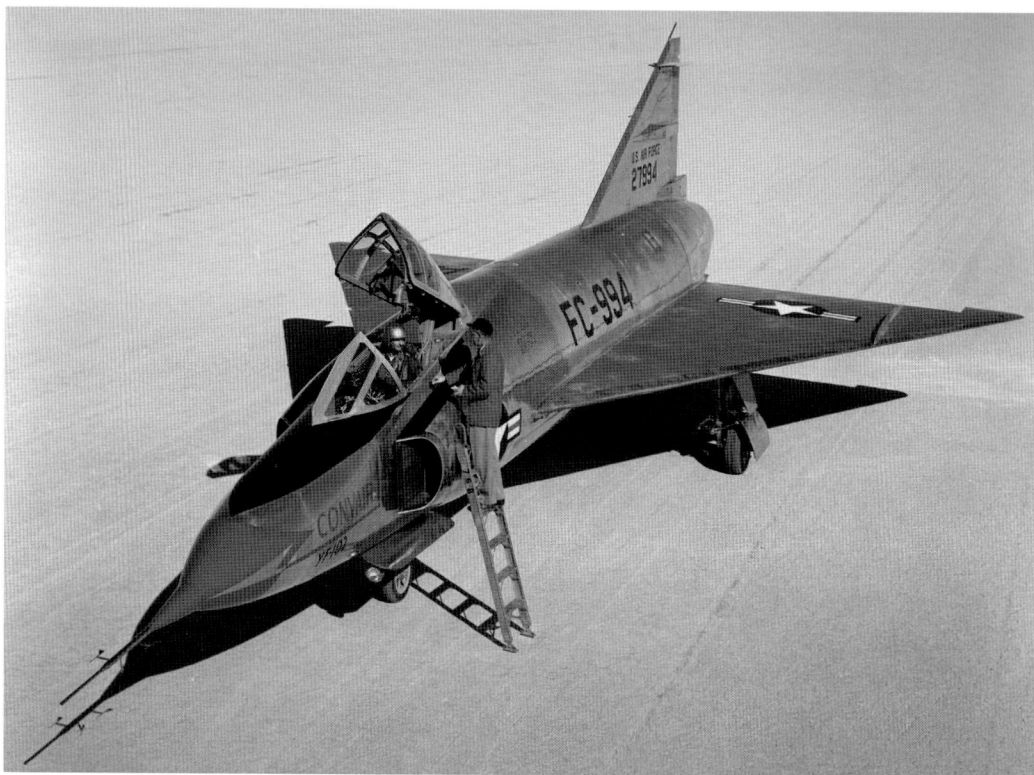

Above: The first of ten YF-102s, 52-7994, is during early flight testing at Rogers Dry Lake, Edwards AFB, in late October 1953. (*General Dynamics (Convair Division)/Richard Ward Collection*)

Below: The sixth Convair YF-102, 53-1782 'FC-782', which at this stage of the aircraft's development looked little different to the XF-92 from a NACA 'area-rule' point of view. (*Richard Ward Collection*)

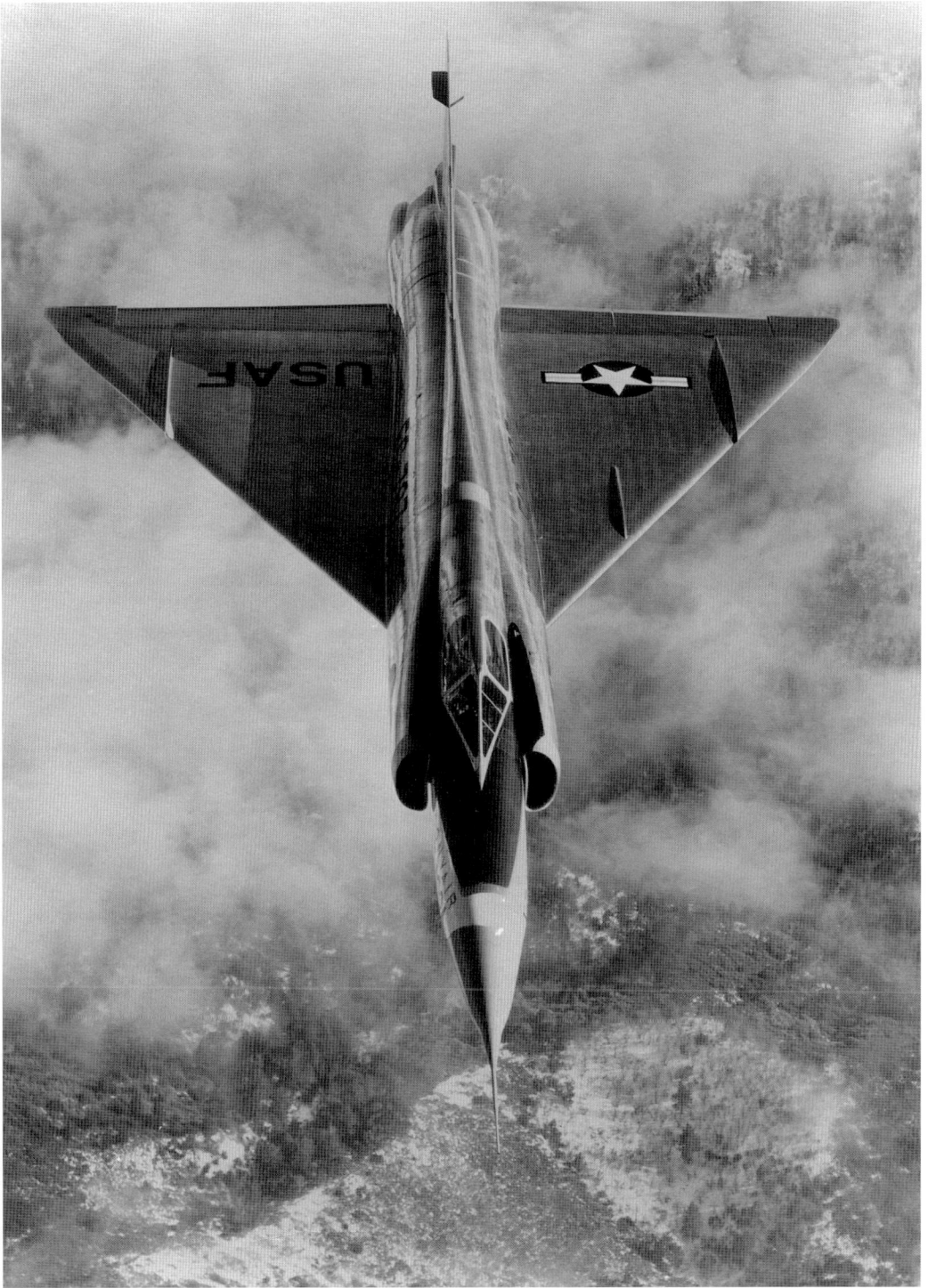

The area rule or 'coke-bottle' shaped fuselage dramatically changed the appearance and performance of the YF-102A. This is the first of four YF-102As, 53-1787, flown for the first time on 2 December 1954. (*General Dynamics (Convair Division)/Richard Ward Collection*)

A lovely study of a crisp and clean F-102A Delta Dagger. Like so many other F-102s, 56-1041 enjoyed a long service career with the 498th FIS, 318th FIS, 199th FIS (Hawaii ANG) and the 118th FIS before being delivered to the AMARC 'bone yard' in April 1970. Not long after, the aircraft was delivered to the New Mexico Institute of Technology and Mining at Socorro for explosive testing and was finally scrapped in 1975. (*General Dynamics (Convair Division)/ Richard Ward Collection*)

The F-102A was also used in the close support role over South Vietnam from 1965, under Project Stovepipe. Operating over the Ho Chi Minh trail, the aircraft's heat-seeking Falcon missiles were used on heat sources at night, which were usually thought to be Viet Cong campfires. The tactic was literally hit and miss, as the pilots firing the missiles were never sure if anything had been hit, and Stovepipe was only ever seen as a harassment tactic. The F-102A was also operated during the day against ground targets, making use of the FFAR rockets on 618 sorties up to late 1965.

Not a single air-to-air combat was fought with the enemy during this period, although one F-102A of 509th FIS was shot down by a MiG-21 during a CAP over Route Package IV on 3 February 1968. Only fifteen F-102s were lost during the Vietnam War before the type was withdrawn from South East Asia in December 1969. Two of them were attributed to anti-aircraft or small arms fire, four were destroyed on the ground and eight more were lost in operational accidents.

Back in the USA, the F-102A was already being steadily replaced on ACD units by the F-101B Voodoo and the F-106A Delta Dart. By the summer of 1961, F-102A strength was down to 221 and, by 1969, with the exception of a single ADC unit in Iceland, all had been transferred to the ANG (Air National Guard).

Above: The very first TF-102 Delta Dagger two-seat trainer, which made its maiden flight on 18 November 1955. After service with the 4780th ADW the aircraft was converted to a GTF-102A and continued to serve with the 78th FIS. The aircraft can be seen at the Selfridge Military Air Museum in Michigan. (*General Dynamics (Convair Division)/Richard Ward Collection*)

Below: F-102A-5-CO 53-1793 launching twenty-four 2.75 in. (70 mm) unguided FFARs in around 1957. (*General Dynamics (Convair Division)/Richard Ward Collection*)

Above: F-102A 56-1127 in service with the last of seven operational units, namely the 157th FIS, South Carolina ANG, at McEntire ANGB. Converted into a PQM-102B, this loyal machine was shot down over the Gulf of Mexico on 20 August 1980. (*Richard Ward Collection*)

Below: A 49th FIS F-102A from an unusual angle during the biennial William Tell aerial gunnery competition in 1982; that year the event was held at Tyndall AFB. (*Richard Ward Collection*)

Above: Greece purchased nineteen F-102As and five TF-102As in 1969, including this machine, 0-60981 (56-981). These aircraft served until 1978 and this particular aircraft is believed to be in storage at Elefsis AB. (*Richard Ward Collection*)

Below: PQM-102A 56-1061 '656/24' pictured in 1979, not long before the aircraft crashed on landing at Holloman AFB on 13 November. (*Richard Ward Collection*)

By 1970, the only aircraft operating on USAF strength were with West German and Netherlands-based units. However, not long after, these units were destined to replace the F-102As with the F-4 Phantom, leaving the 57th FIS at Keflavik, Iceland, to become the last of its kind. The 199th FIS, Hawaii ANG, was the last unit to operate the F-102A which saw its 'Deuces' replaced by the F-4C in October 1976. It had been an uncomfortable and often fragile beginning for the F-102A, which continued to be modified throughout its service career, eventually maturing into one of the USAF's most popular aircraft.

111 trainer versions of the F-102, complete with side-by-side cockpits and full operational capability, were also built, designated as the TF-102A (Model 8-12). Half a dozen F-102As were converted into target drones to represent MiG-21s in April 1973 and designated as the QF-102A. It was as drones that F-102s would pay their final service to the USAF in the shape of sixty-five PQM-102As and 146 PQM-102Bs. The former were unpiloted drones and that latter could be operated remotely or with a pilot in the cockpit. The bulk of these PQMs were 'despatched' over test ranges. Also worthy of mention was Convair's efforts to improve the Delta Dagger in the shape of the F-102B; this machine would later become the F-106 Delta Dart.

F2Y Sea Dart

The first generation jets of the late 1940s and early 1950s were only a little more powerful than their piston-powered predecessors and the US Navy, in particular, was struggling to transition to the new power plant. Doubting whether supersonic jet-powered fighters would ever operate effectively from their carriers, the US Navy began to show interest in a seaplane fighter. Having already created (to model stage) a jet-powered seaplane called the Skate, Convair came up with a new proposal which was named the Sea Dart (Model 2).

On 19 November 1951, Convair's proposal was accepted by the US Navy and the company was contracted to produce a pair of prototypes designated the XF2Y-1 Sea Dart. A fascinating design, the Sea Dart had a vee-shaped hull complete with water-tight compartments should the aircraft be damaged in combat. The Sea Dart also had a delta-wing configuration and a large surface area fin. The engines were mounted on top of the fuselage and to the rear, the intakes being positioned as far away as possible from the water to prevent ingestion. The undercarriage was a pair of hydro-skis which provided enough hydrodynamic lift to raise the fuselage above the waterline on take-off.

The US Navy were very keen on the Sea Dart, to such a degree that an order was placed for four evaluation aircraft designated the YF2Y-1 and a dozen production aircraft, designated the F2Y-1, on 28 August 1952, long before the first XF2Y-1, 137634, took to the air.

The prototype XF2Y-1 Sea Dart, 137634, taking to the air in 1954. (*US Navy/Richard Ward Collection*)

The US Navy was very excited by the concept of the Sea Dart, to such a degree that they placed an order for two prototypes, four evaluation aircraft and a dozen pre-production machines. In the end only five aircraft were built. (*General Dynamics (Convair Division)/Richard Ward Collection*)

It was always the intention to install a pair of 6,000 lb Westinghouse XJ46 engines in the aircraft but, by the time the prototype was approaching completion, only the 3,400 lb J34 was available. Regardless, taxi trials began in December 1953 in San Diego Bay and, on 9 April 1953, in the hands of 'Sam' Shannon, the Sea Dart took to the air for the first time. The lack of power from the J34s saw the Sea Dart remain staunchly sub-sonic and the hydro-skis made for a rough ride. The latter was marginally resolved and the XJ46 (J46) engines were installed later in 1953.

The second prototype was cancelled and the programme moved on to the first evaluation, YF2Y-1, 135762, which was installed with J46 engines. Flight testing began again in 1954 and one particular success of that year was when test pilot Charles E. Richbourg broke the sound barrier in a shallow dive on 3 August 1954 (the only seaplane ever to achieve such a record). Unfortunately, Richbourg was to publically lose his life in 135762 on 4 November 1954 during a demonstration to the press. By this stage, the US Navy was already losing interest and the original contract had been chopped back to a handful of aircraft. Convair continued on, modifying and improving as it went, but by April 1955, when the last Sea Dart flight was carried out, jet engines had been dramatically improved and the US Navy was more confident in the operation of supersonic aircraft aboard its carriers.

In the end, only five aircraft were built and, luckily enough, most likely thanks to its unique design, four of them, including the first prototype, survive to this day, all of them in the USA.

Above: The ingenious design, including the hydro-skis, is clearly evident in this view of F2Y-1 Sea Dart 135762 in around 1954. (*US Navy/Richard Ward Collection*)

Below: One of the four Sea Dart survivors is YF2Y-1 135765, which today resides at the Florida Air Museum in Florida. (*Richard Ward Collection*)

XFY-1 'Pogo'

'Outside of the box' thinking was rife in the US military during the late 1940s and early 1950s and an example of this was a US Navy proposal for a fighter capable of performing a vertical take-off and landing. Two companies presented plausible designs; one of them was Lockheed with its XFV-1 and the other was Convair with the XFY-1 (Model 5), which would later be nicknamed 'Pogo'; both would be given contracts to produce these amazing machines.

The US Navy wanted an aircraft that could operate from small platforms onboard ships and, as such, the machine would be sitting on its tail in a true VTOL configuration. These VTOL fighters would be ideal for protecting military vessels that did not have the luxury of a carrier nearby. Contracts were awarded to Convair and Lockheed in May 1951 with instructions to produce at least a pair of experimental fighters apiece. Convair planned to build three XFY-1s serialled 138648 to 138650; however, only 138649 was destined to fly, while the first aircraft would be employed as an engine test bed and the last would be used for static testing.

The unique XFY-1 'Pogo', 138648, pictured en route to Moffett Field where extensive ground testing (inside a massive airship hangar) would take place in April 1954. (*General Dynamics (Convair Division)/Richard Ward Collection*)

The XFY-1 sits 'precariously' on an experimental launching ramp which was never tested or put into practice. (*General Dynamics (Convair Division)/Richard Ward Collection*)

An unusual looking aircraft, the XFY-1 had a short, deep fuselage which was effectively wrapped around a powerful Allison turboprop. The aircraft was actually designed for the YT40-A-14, which developed 7,100 hp, but would fly with the less powerful 5,850 hp YT40-A-6. Ambitious plans for the production aircraft included the installation of the even more powerful Allison T54 but this unit was never built and history dictated that the highly successful T56 would pave the way instead, none of which affected the future outcome of the XFY-1. At the sharp end of the Allison turboprop was a complex set of Curtiss-Wright co-axial contra-rotating propellers, each unit with a trio of 16-foot-long blades. The pilot's cockpit was perched on top of the fuselage and, in order to help him deal with this unusual configuration, the seat was mounted on gimbals, which meant that it could be placed at an angle of 45 degrees while in the vertical and a normal 90 degrees in level flight. The wings were a delta shape, while the large tail surfaces extended equally in a dorsal and ventral arrangement. The undercarriage was little more than castoring wheels positioned on extended poles at four points on the wing tips and tail surfaces.

The bizarre looking XFY-1 was rolled out in early 1954 and, within days, was on the road to Moffett Field to begin extensive ground testing. The tests were carried out inside an airship hangar at Moffett under tethered conditions with Convair test pilot Lt-Col. James F. 'Skeets' Coleman at the controls. Testing a machine like this was seriously new territory and every effort was made to ensure Coleman's safety during these early trials. As such, the propeller hub was removed and a pair of cables were attached to the roof of the hangar, which was 198 feet high, while below four more cables were attached to the undercarriage points. All of the cables were controlled by ground engineer Bob McGreary, who could activate a winch to take the strain of the XFY-1 should Coleman lose control. It was the perfect 'belt and braces' set up and it worked very well. Coleman carried out the first tethered test on 19 April 1954. Progress was swift from this point but it still took every ounce of Coleman's skill and experience to control the XFY-1. With nearly 60 hours of testing under his belt, it was decided to operate the aircraft outside for the first time in late July. On 1 August, the first of two proper flight tests took place, the second up to an altitude of 150 feet. On both occasions, the XFY-1 took off vertically and was landed vertically. The latter, even with the seat at an angle of 45 degrees, involved Coleman straining to look over his shoulder to make sure that the aircraft was in the right position before touchdown. Coleman soon mastered the XFY-1 and in a short space of time built up an impressive seventy take-offs and landings without incident and, on 2 November 1954, transitioned to horizontal flight for the first time. For this incredible flight, Coleman was awarded the Harmon Trophy.

Although the XFY-1's maximum speed fell well short of the new generation of jet fighters, the aircraft was still something of a 'hot ship' thanks to lack of flaps or spoilers to slow the machine down after a high-speed run. (*General Dynamics (Convair Division)/ Richard Ward Collection*)

With Lt-Col. James F 'Skeets' Coleman at the controls, the XFY-1 is slowly brought back down to earth in a vertical descent. Note how Coleman is straining to look over his left shoulder to locate his landing spot. (*General Dynamics (Convair Division)/Richard Ward Collection*)

XFY-1 'Pogo' 138649 at rest at NAS Norfolk, Virginia; today the aircraft is on display at the Udvvar/Hazy Centre of the National Air and Space Museum. (*Richard Ward Collection*)

As with all test programmes, regular flight testing would expose general design issues and the XFY-1 was no exception. One of the practical issues was the aircraft's phenomenal power to weight ratio, which was fine on paper but a different story when trying to slow the machine down for a landing. The aircraft was not fitted with flaps, spoilers or any kind of air brake so the landing had to be planned in the same manner as a forward-thinking super tanker captain! Overall performance of the aircraft was good but more traditionally designed fighters which could fly twice as fast were already being looked at by the US Navy. Flight testing continued into 1955 at Lindbergh Field, San Diego, but on 1 August of that year the project was brought to an end after XFY-1 138649 had chalked up 40 flying hours.

While the two ground test airframes were later scrapped, 138649 was for many years placed on static display at NAS Norfolk, Virginia. Later, the aircraft was moved into storage at the Paul Garber facility, Suitland, before moving again to the Udvvar/Hazy Centre of the National Air and Space Museum, where it can be seen to this day.

B-58 Hustler

The USAF's Air Research and Development Command (ARDC) invited US aircraft manufacturers to tender ideas for a supersonic bomber in March 1949. Multiple submissions were made but only two were taken seriously by the ARDC, one proposal from Boeing and another from Convair's Fort Worth Division. In August 1952, the latter design was selected with the title Convair Model 4, to be built under Contract MX-1964. The designation B-58 was allocated on 10 December 1952 and, before the year was over, a contract to build eighteen aircraft was received, all of which were to be powered by the brand new General Electric J79 turbojet, which was still under development.

The demand for supersonic performance would push the envelope on multiple levels, including advanced aerodynamics, structure and new materials. The B-58 would become the first aircraft to take advantage of the NACA/Whitcomb area-rule concept. The result was a striking delta-winged aircraft with four underslung engines in pods, a very narrow fuselage and an unusual 75-foot-long under-fuselage pod which could carry additional fuel and at least one nuclear weapon or a weapons load up to 19,450 lb in weight. The crew was made up of a pilot, an observer and a Defence System Operator (DSO). The observer also served as the navigator, radar operator and bombardier while the DSO was also an assistant to the pilot and operated the ECM equipment. Each crewman had his own individual cockpit and a jettisonable escape capsule.

The eighteen aircraft in the contract were reduced to thirteen aircraft in June 1954, made up of a pair of XB-58 prototypes and eleven YB-58A pre-production machines. The first of these aircraft,

The first of two pre-production YB-58As was 55-660, which first flew on 11 November 1957. Christened *Old Grandpappy*, this ground-breaking prototype was unceremoniously scrapped at Kelly AFB in early 1960. (*General Dynamics (Convair Division)/Richard Ward Collection*)

Employing the same area-rule approach that elevated the performance of the F-102, the B-58 was the world's fastest bomber when it entered USAF service in late 1959. (*General Dynamics (Convair Division)/Richard Ward Collection*)

XB-58 55-660, was rolled out at Fort Worth on 31 August 1958 and on 11 November of that year made its maiden flight in the hands of Beryl A. Erickson. Up to this point, the XB-58 was yet to be installed with its main weapons pod, of which thirty-one were initially ordered. In this clean configuration, the XB-58 became the first bomber to break the sound barrier, on 30 December 1958. In the meantime, the initial order of YB-58As was increased by a further seventeen, making a total of thirty aircraft available for manufacturer's trials and ARDC trials. The latter would be carried out by the 6592nd Test Squadron and the 3958th Operational Evaluation and Training Squadron at Carswell AFB.

The USAF ordered a total of eighty-six B-58A Hustlers between September 1958 and 1960 plus ten YB-58As which were modified to production standard. Total production would reach 116 aircraft, including eight TB-58A trainers. Initially, the bomber was assigned to the 43rd BW at Carswell, which later moved to Little Rock, and the 30th BW at Bunker Hill. The first of the production machines was delivered to the 65th Combat Crew Training Squadron at Carswell on 1 December 1959 while the 43rd BW became the first fully operational B-58 unit on 15 March 1960.

B-58A-15-CF Hustler 60-1116 under construction at Fort Worth. Twenty-six B-58s were lost in various accidents, including 60-1116, which was written off when the undercarriage collapsed at Bunker Hill while assigned to the 305th BW. (*General Dynamics (Convair Division)/Richard Ward Collection*)

The Fort Worth production line in full swing; total production (at approximately $12.5 million each) reached 116 aircraft between 1958 and 1960. (*General Dynamics (Convair Division)/ Richard Ward Collection*)

B-58A 61-2059 *Can Do*, which flew 8,028 miles from Tokyo to London on 16 October 1963 in 8½ hours at an average speed of 938 mph. The aircraft is preserved at the Strategic Aerospace Museum at Offutt AFB. (*Richard Ward Collection*)

A nice view of a B-58A complete with the 75-foot-long MB-1C under-fuselage pod. The pod had multiple bays from front to back for equipment, a forward fuel tank, a thermonuclear weapons bay, a rear fuel tank and finally a tail cone. (*General Dynamics (Convair Division)/Richard Ward Collection*)

The 1960s was ripe for record-breaking and the high-performing B-58 Hustler had all the ingredients needed. The first to fall was the 1,243 mile (2,000 km) closed-circuit record on 12 January 1961, when Major Henry Deutschendorf and crew recorded a speed of 1,061.8 mph. Two days later, the 621 mile (1,000 km) closed-circuit record was raised to an eye-watering 1,284.75 mph by Major Harold E. Confer and crew. Another B-58 crew, captained by Major Elmer Murphy, won the Louis Bleriot Trophy by becoming the first pilot to exceed 1,242.75 mph (2,000 kmh) for 30 minutes straight! In all, the impressive B-58 set nineteen world speed records and it is of little wonder that a lot of ex-Hustler crews were chosen to fly the Lockheed SR-71A Blackbird.

The B-58 was an expensive machine to buy and just as expensive to operate; as such, its operational career was short. On 27 October 1969, the Secretary of Defence announced a number of cuts which included the closure of Little Rock and Bunker Hill and the removal from the inventory of the B-58 wings. Within days, the first B-58s were being flown to Davis-Monthan for storage and by the end of 1970 this impressive machine had been quickly erased from the USAF.

F-106 Delta Dart

While the F-102A Delta Dagger entered service with the USAF as an interim, Convair continued working hard to build the 'ultimate interceptor', focussing on the F-102B. The latter would have considerably improved performance, a Hughes MA-1 fire-control system and an array of new equipment. In November 1955, the USAF placed an order for seventeen F-102Bs, an aircraft which was so far removed from the original F-102 that it was re-designated as the F-106A on 17 June 1956. By then, the expectation of this 'ultimate interceptor' had increased somewhat and the USAF's criteria, presented on 28 September 1956, required that the new fighter be capable of intercepting enemy aircraft up to 70,000 feet and up to a radius of 430 miles. Armed with guided missiles and/or rockets with atomic warheads, the new F-106 was required to carry these missions out at speeds of up to Mach 2 and up to 35,000 feet using a guidance system known as SAGE (Semi-Automatic Guidance Environment) which integrated with the MA-1 system.

YF-106A (Model 8-24) 56-451 was the first of the breed to fly from Edwards on 26 December 1956 with Convair Chief Test Pilot Richard L. 'Dick' Johnson in the hot seat. During the first flight, Johnson took the YF-106A to Mach 1.9 and a height of 57,000 feet, which was impressive but still well short of

The first production F-106A Delta Dart, 56-451, touches down at Edwards AFB after its maiden flight on 26 December 1956. This aircraft is preserved at the Selfridge Military Air Museum. (*General Dynamics (Convair Division)/Richard Ward Collection*)

The second production F-106A, 56-452, which ended its days as a ground trainer at Amarillo AFB. (*USAF/Richard Ward Collection*)

the USAF requirements for their 'ultimate interceptor'. This was still a significant performance increase over the original F-102A, thanks mainly to the installation of the more powerful Pratt & Whitney J75 engine. This power plant required a redesigned variable-geometry air intake which controlled the amount of air that the engine needed across a wide range of supersonic speeds. Leading up to the installation of the J75, the F-106A was on shaky ground, not helped by the MA-1 system failing to perform as well as expected and the more worrying fact that the USAF was running out of funds to throw at the project.

The USAF had always planned to order 1,000 F-106s but, in an effort to gain something from a rapidly deteriorating situation, the order was reduced to 350 aircraft. Further tweaks and modifications saw the F-106 mature quickly and the first production machines were ready for delivery in October 1959, the first recipient being the 498th FIS at Geiger AFB. Sixty-three F-106Bs (Model 8-27) also made up the total order; these two-seat trainers still retained a fully operational capability.

Even before production had ended, a large modification programme was introduced so that all F-106As and F-106Bs served the USAF to a common standard. As a result, the F-106A became the Model 8-31 and the F-106B the Model 8-32. The F-106 served the USAF for much longer than expected and it was not until 1981 that the F-106 began to be replaced by the F-15 Eagle, although a number remained in service with second-line units and the ANG until 1988 and one F-106B served with NASA until 1991. As with the F-102, a number of F-106s were converted into target drones and redesignated as the QF-106A. 194 F-106s were converted and the last of them served until 1997.

Above: A typically well turned-out F-106A (59-0091) of the 87th FIS based at K. I. Sawyer AFB in Michigan. Retired to MASDC on 15 January 1985, this aircraft was converted into a QF-106 ('AD254') and was shot down by an AIM-7M air-to-air missile on 15 July 1994. (*Richard Ward Collection*)

Below: A pair of 498th FIS F-106Bs climb out of Geiger Field, Washington. The nearest machine, 0-90162, crashed on 9 February 1971. (*Harry Walker/Richard Ward Collection*)

Still looking good in its twilight years, this F-106B, 59-0161, is pictured in 1982. Two years after this image was taken the aircraft was retired to MASDC and was later converted into a QF-106 ('AD280'). This beautiful aircraft's long career came to an abrupt end on 22 January 1997 when it was despatched by an AIM-120 air-air-missile. (*Richard Ward Collection*)

CV-880 and 990

The 1950s was a busy and rapidly changing decade when it came to air transport and both Boeing and Douglas were investing a great deal of time and money in creating the first generation of turbojet-powered airliners. Convair wanted its slice of this potentially lucrative pie but instead of creating a similar alternative for the airline industry, in true style, they decided to offer something a little different. Having carried out its own market research, Convair came up with a design that would carry fewer passengers than the Boeing 707 and Douglas DC-8 but would deliver them faster.

Convair announced in April 1956 that it was ready to join the turbojet airliner market and at the same time delivered the encouraging news that Delta Air Lines had ordered ten aircraft and TWA thirty. Designated by the company as the Model 22, the aircraft initially had a number of names such as the Convair Skylark, later changed to Golden Arrow, the Convair 600 and finally the Convair 880.

The aircraft was not dissimilar, on the surface, to the Boeing 707 in its general configuration. A large, low-wing monoplane with a wing that had a 35 degree sweep and turbojet engines housed in pods

The very first Convair 880 (880-22-1), N801TW, which first flew on 27 January 1959. This striking-looking airliner went to serve with Northeast, TWA, American Jet Industries, Gulfstream American, Gulfstream Aerospace and Charlotte Aerospace. The cockpit of this aircraft can be seen at the Delta Flight Museum, Atlanta. (*General Dynamics (Convair Division)/ Richard Ward Collection*)

Delta Air Lines operated seventeen CV-880s including N8802E, which served the airline from 2 October 1960 to 1973. (*General Dynamics (Convair Division)/Richard Ward Collection*)

under the wing. All tail surfaces were swept in a traditional arrangement while the undercarriage consisted of twin wheels under the nose and a pair of four-wheel bogie units serving as the main. Apart from a differently stepped nose, the key difference between the Convair 880 and the Boeing 707 was that the former had a narrower fuselage. This meant that the Convair machine could only manage a five-abreast layout which gave room for between eighty-eight and 110 passengers while the Boeing was six abreast and could seat up to 189 passengers.

The first Convair 880, registered as N801TW, made its maiden flight on 27 January 1959 with Don Germeraad in the left-hand seat and Phil Prophett in the right. Intended for domestic use, the Convair 880 gained its official FAA certification on 1 May 1960 and, just two weeks later, Delta Air Lines flew its first service with the new airliner. This optimistic period was short-lived for the Convair 880 and orders soon dried up as operators realised that the Boeing and Douglas were still better options. Only forty-eight Convair 880s were built and, in an attempt to revive sales, a new model with greater fuel capacity and a wealth of other improvements was introduced. This was the Convair 880M (Model 31) but the fundamental problem of a lack passenger seats remained and only seventeen of these were sold.

Convair had every intention of creating a higher-capacity, better performing aircraft long before the 880 had even flown. This was designated as the Model 30, an aircraft that American Airlines placed an order for at a very early stage. That stage was reached long before negative customer reaction to the Convair 880 and if the company had known this information in advance, they would never have proceeded with the Model 30 in its current five-abreast seating layout. Named the Convair 990, this new

CV-880-22M-21 N112 was operated by the Federal Aviation Administration for many years before being sold to Flight Systems. The aircraft was then operated by the US Navy as a UC-880 as part of cruise missile testing before being retired on 30 September 1993. By now serialled as 161572, this was the last flight of a CV-880. (*General Dynamics (Convair Division)/Richard Ward Collection*)

machine had a lengthened fuselage that raised passenger capacity to a maximum of 149, which was still well-short of its direct competitors.

The first Convair 990, registered as N5601 and built for American Airlines, made its maiden flight in the hands of Don Germeraad on 24 January 1961. Certification was not received until December 1961 and it was American Airlines who took the 990 into service first on 7 January 1962. Swissair was also interested in the 990 and it took the aircraft into service in February 1962, naming the airliner the Coronado.

The reason that the Convair 990 took so long to gain its certification was because a number of modifications needed to be made before the aircraft could enter service. Many of these problems revolved around aerodynamics and it was not until modification work to the engine pods and the installation of full-span flaps that the 990 was good to go. Such was the number of changes that the aircraft was redesignated as the 990A and all aircraft produced, just thirty-seven, were retrospectively modified to this standard. The higher cruising speed and longer range introduced by the Convair 990 was too little too late.

This last problem was enough for General Dynamics and the plug was pulled, bringing to an end an exercise which cost millions of dollars with nothing to show for it. Infamously, the Convair 880 and 990 story proved to be the most financially damaging production line in the history of aviation and General Dynamics would never venture into the civilian market place again. This would prove to be the beginning of the end for Convair as a result.

Above: A pair of Convair engineers pose for the camera and 'tinker' with the starboard outer General Electric CJ-805 turbojet of a CV-880. (*General Dynamics (Convair Division)/Richard Ward Collection*)

Below: Originally delivered to American Airlines back in May 1962, this CV-990-30A Coronado went on to join NASA and was modified into a Landing Systems Research Aircraft. (*NASA (EC93-41018-12)*)

Model 48 Charger

Convair's final design, and one of its most controversial aircraft, was the Model 48 Charger which was designed to meet a complex, yet ground-breaking, specification for a COIN (Counter Insurgency) aircraft.

The idea for a small aircraft which could operate from short strips or roads close behind the front line and provide close air support was first muted by a couple of USMC officers in 1959. The seed was sown, interest began to grow and, in 1961, Convair began a serious design study into COIN machines. By 1963, the USMC, the US Army and the US Navy were all interested in the concept and as a result a tri-service set of specifications was sent out to a number of major aircraft manufacturers under the name LARA (Light Armed Reconnaissance Aircraft).

The sole Charger prototype, with the civilian registration N28K, looks an impressive sight with a wide range of offensive, defensive and fuel tank options. (*General Dynamics (Convair Division)/Richard Ward Collection*)

Convair presented the Model 48 Charger as part of the LARA competition in March 1964. With the Charger taking shape in the background, note the diminutive yet powerful T74 turboprop in the foreground. (*General Dynamics (Convair Division)/Richard Ward Collection*)

No fewer than nine manufacturers began working on the idea, including Convair, who presented the Model 48 Charger in March 1964. The Charger had a novel arrangement with twin booms leading back from its twin T74 turboprop engines, a very short wing and a central pod containing the crew with a cargo area to the rear. The aircraft's nose, rear fuselage and wingtips were made from fibreglass and the aircraft had a retractable tricycle undercarriage. With a wing span of just 27 feet 6 inches, most of the surface was affected by the slipstream of the aircraft's engines, which drove a pair of three-blade Hamilton Standard propellers with 8 foot 6 inch blades. The wing had full-span trailing edge slotted flaps and leading edge slats which took full advantage of the slipstream to such a degree that the take-off and landing run was incredibly short. The combination of the inboard leading edge slats and the trailing edge slats almost produced a form of vectored thrust that gave the aircraft potentially superb short-field performance, which was a major tick in the box of the LARA specification. The Charger was also fitted with a large, 20-foot span all-moving tailplane which sat on top of the fins.

The pilot and observer were housed in tandem configuration under a large sliding canopy fielding excellent visibility. The rear of the central pod was taken up by a cargo bay which was accessed from the rear via a hinged tail cone. 2,000 lb of cargo could be carried and there was even enough room for a spare T74 engine if needed. An alternative roll for the cargo bay was to carry paratroops, of which there was room for five, although apparently a sixth could be shoehorned into the observer's seat. All in all, the Charger fitted the LARA specification perfectly and had the potential to perform better.

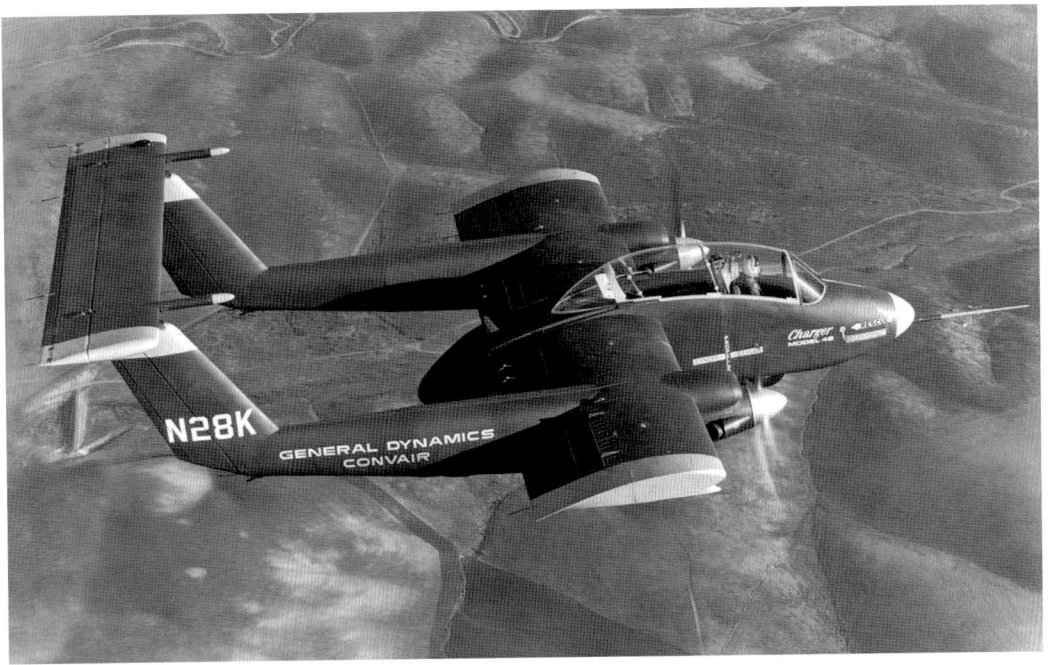

Above: The Charger was a lively performer, with a maximum speed of 319 mph thanks to its 650 hp T74-CP-8/10 (PT-6) turboprops. (*General Dynamics (Convair Division)/Richard Ward Collection*)

Below: A good angle to see how 'busy' the wing of the Charger was and how crucial it was for the STOL performance required of the LARA specification. Note the lack of equipment (including a seat) in the observer's rear-seat position. (*General Dynamics (Convair Division)/Richard Ward Collection*)

With a wing span of just 27 feet 6 inches, the Charger did not need a great deal of room to operate and with a standard payload could be off the ground and over a 50-foot obstacle in a distance of just 485 feet. (*General Dynamics (Convair Division)/Richard Ward Collection*)

Without waiting for the winner of the LARA competition to be announced, Convair began construction of a single prototype as a private venture which resulted in the civilian serial N28K being allocated, from design to maiden flight taking a mere thirty-five weeks. However, in the meantime the US Navy, to many somewhat prematurely, announced in August 1964 that the winner of the LARA competition was the North American NA-300, more familiarly known as the OV-10 Bronco. Neither the US Army nor the USMC were happy, both of them preferring the Charger, which made its maiden flight in the hands of John W. Knebel on 25 November 1964.

From the outset the Charger was a great performer and, after several modifications, which included a greater wing span and much improved tailplane, the aircraft just got better. With a standard payload, the Charger cleared a 50-foot obstacle in just 485 feet, which was almost half of what the LARA specification called for! More importantly, the Charger performed much better than the Bronco. Not all was lost for Convair as the aircraft managed to gain a 100-hour flight test contract which would see test pilots from the USAF, US Navy, USMC and US Army fly the Charger. With a potential order still a possibility, hopes were high at Convair but sadly these were dashed on 19 October 1965 when a US Navy test pilot lost control of the machine on its 196th test flight and was forced to eject at low level. Put down to pilot error, the individual survived while the Charger was completely destroyed, bringing to an end any further hope of a production and no more wonderful designs from the Convair stable.

Technical Information

Engines

Type	Power Plant
XA-41	One 3,000 hp P&W R-4360 Wasp Major
XP-81	One 2,300 ehp GE XT31-GE-1 (TG-100) and one 3,750 lbs.t. Allison J33-GE-5
L-13	(Prototype) One 245 hp Franklin O-425-6; (Production) one Franklin 250 hp O-425-9
XB/YB-36/A	Six 3,000 hp P&W R-4360-25 Wasp Major
B-36B/D	Six 3,500 hp P&W R-4360-41 Wasp Major
B-36F/J/H	Six 3,800 hp R-4360-53 Wasp Major
B-36D/F/J	Plus four 5,200 lbs.t. GE J47-GE-19 turbojets
Model 106	One 230 hp Franklin 6A8-225-B8
Model 111	One 65 hp Continental A-65
Model 116	One 90 hp Franklin 4A4 or 4AG or 95 hp 4AL and one 26 hp Crosley
Model 118	One 190 hp Lycoming O-435C air-cooled and one 26 hp Crosley
Model 108	One 165 hp Franklin 6A4
Model 110	Two 2,100 hp P&W R-2800-2SC13 Wasp
CV-240	Two 2,400 hp P&W R-2800-CA3/15/18 or CB3/16 Wasp
T-29A	Two 2,400 hp P&W R-2800-97
T-29C	Two 2,500 hp P&W R-2800-99W
CV-340/440	Two 2,500 hp P&W R-2800-CB16 or CB17
C-131B	Two 2,500 hp P&W R-2800-99
CC-109	Two 3,500 ehp Napier Eland
CV-540	Two 3,060 ehp Eland NEI.1
CV-640	Two 3,025 ehp Rolls-Royce RDa.10/1 Dart
XB-46	Four 4,000 lb Allison-built GE TG-180 (J35)
XC-99	Six 3,500 hp P&W R-4360-41 Wasp Major
XF-92A	One 7,500 lb (wet) Allison J33-A-29
R3Y	Four 5,850 hp Allison T40-A-10
YB-60	Eight 8,700 lb P&W J57-P-3
F-102A	One 17,200 lb (wet) P&W J57-P-23
F2Y	(Prototype) Two 3,400 lb Westinghouse J34-WE-32; Two 6,000 lb J46-WE-2
XFY-1	One 5,850 hp Allison YT40-A-6
B-58A	Four 15,000 lb (wet) GE J79-GE-5A
F-106A	One 24,500 lb (wet) Pratt & Whitney J75-P-17
CV-880	Four 11,650 lb GE CJ-805-3B
CV-990	Four 16,050 lb GE CJ805-23B
Model 48	Two 650 hp P&W-Canada T74-CP-8/10 (PT-6)

Performance

Type	Max Speed	Cruise	Climb Rate	Service Ceiling	Range (miles)
XA-41	363 mph	–	2,730 ft/min.	27,000 ft	800
XP-81	507 mph	–	5,300 ft/min.	35,500 ft	2,500
L-13	115 mph	92 mph	–	15,000 ft	368
B-36A	345 mph	218 mph	1,447 ft/min.	39,100 ft	3,880*
B-36B	381 mph	202 mph	1,510 ft/min.	42,500 ft	3,740*
B-36D	439 mph	225 mph	2,210 ft/min.	45,200 ft	3,525*
B-36F	417 mph	235 mph	2,060 ft/min.	44,000 ft	3,200*
B-36H	439 mph	234 mph	2,060 ft/min.	44,000 ft	3,113*
B-36J	411 mph	203 mph	1,920 ft/min.	39,900 ft	6,800*
Model 106	142 mph	–	–	–	–
Model 116	112.5 mph	–	–	–	–
Model 118	125 mph	–	–	–	–
Model 108	143 mph	121 mph	–	–	–
Model 110	314 mph	260 mph	–	–	850
CV-240	315 mph	280 mph	–	16,000 ft	1,200
C-131B	293 mph	254 mph	–	24,500 ft	1,790
CC-109	340 mph	322 mph	–	25,300 ft	2,275
CV-440	–	300 mph	–	24,900 ft	1,930
T-29A	–	–	–	–	2,550
CV-640	–	300 mph	–	–	1,950
XB-46	565 mph	–	–	43,000 ft	2,500
XC-99	307 mph	–	–	30,000 ft	8,100
XF-92A	718 mph	–	8,135 ft/min.	50,750 ft	–
R3Y	403 mph	300 mph	–	39,700 ft	4,000
YB-60	508 mph	–	1,570 ft/min.	44,650 ft**	2,920
F-102A	825 mph	–	13,000 ft/min.	53,400 ft	1,350
F2Y	695 mph***	–	32,700 ft/min.***	54,800 ft***	513
XFY-1	610 mph	–	10,500 ft/min.	43,700 ft	–
B-58A	1,319 mph	–	17,400 ft/min.	63,400 ft	–
F-106A	1,525 mph	–	–	57,000 ft	1,600****
CV-880	–	610 mph	–	41,000 ft	3,385
CV-990A	621 mph	557 mph	–	41,000 ft	3,595
Model 48	319 mph	–	–	21,300 ft	3,000*****

* Combat radius with a 10,000 lb bombload
** Combat ceiling
*** Estimated
**** Combat range
***** Ferry range

Weights

Type	Empty	Loaded	Combat	Maximum
XA-41	13,400 lb	–	–	24,200 lb
XP81	12,755 lb	19,500 lb	–	24,650 lb
L-13	2,070 lb	–	–	2,900 lb
B-36A	135,020 lb	–	212,800 lb	311,000 lb
B-36B	140,640 lb	–	227,700 lb	311,000 lb
B-36D	161,371 lb	–	250,300 lb	370,000 lb
B-36F	167,647 lb	–	264,300 lb	370,000 lb
B-36H	168,487 lb	–	253,900 lb	370,000 lb
B-36J	171,035 lb	–	266,100 lb	410,000 lb
Model 118	1,524 lb	–	–	2,550 lb
Model 108	1,300 lb	–	–	2,400 lb
Model 110	–	14,870 lb	–	–
CV-240	25,445 lb	–	–	–
CV-440	33,314 lb	–	–	49,000 lb
C-131B	29,248 lb	–	–	47,000 lb
CC-109	32,333 lb	–	–	53,200 lb
CV-640	30,275 lb	–	–	49,000 lb
XB-46	–	–	–	91,000 lb
XC-99	135,232 lb	–	–	320,000 lb
XF-92A	9,078 lb	–	–	14,608 lb
R3Y	–	–	–	175,000 lb
YB-60	153,016 lb	–	–	300,000 lb
F-102A	19,350 lb	–	24,494 lb	31,500 lb
F2Y	12,652 lb	–	–	16,527 lb
XFY-1	11,784 lb	–	–	16,250 lb
B-58A	55,560 lb	–	–	176,890 lb
F-106A	23,646 lb	–	–	41,831 lb
CV-880	94,000 lb	–	–	193,000 lb
CV-990A	120,900 lb	–	–	253,000 lb
Model 48	4,457 lb	–	–	10,460 lb

Dimensions

Type	Span	Length	Height	Wing Area
XA-41	54 ft	48 ft 8 in.	14 ft 6 in.	540 sq/ft
XP-81	50 ft 6 in.	44 ft 10 in.	14 ft	425 sq/ft
L-13	30 ft 5.5 in.	31 ft 9 in.	8 ft 5 in.	270 sq/ft
B-36 (all marks)	230 ft	162 ft 1 in.	46 ft 8 in.	4,772 sq/ft
Model 118	34 ft 5 in.	–	8 ft 4 in.	–
Model 108-2	34 ft	24 ft 6 in.	6 ft 10 in.	–
Model 110	89 ft	71 ft 1 in.	–	–
CV-240/T-29A	91 ft 9 in.	74 ft 8 in.	26 ft 11 in.	817 sq/ft
CV-440/C-131B	105 ft 4 in.	79 ft 2 in.*	28 ft 2 in.	920 sq/ft

CV-640	105 ft 4 in.	81 ft 6 in.	28 ft 2 in.	920 sq/ft
XB-46	113 ft	106 ft	28 ft	–
XC-99	230 ft	182 ft 6 in.	57 ft 6 in.	–
XF-92A	31 ft 4 in.	42 ft 6 in.	17 ft 9 in.	–
R3Y	145 ft 9 in.	139 ft 8 in.	44 ft 10 in.	2,102 sq/ft
YB-60	206 ft	171 ft	60 ft 6 in.	5,239 sq/ft
F-102A	38 ft 1½ in.	68 ft 4½ in.	21 ft 2½ in.	695 sq/ft
F2Y	38 ft 8 in.	52 ft 7 in.	20 ft 9 in.**	563 sq/ft
XFY-1	27 ft 7¾ in.	34 ft 11¾ in.	–	355 sq/ft
B-58A	56 ft 9 in.	96 ft 10 in.	29 ft 11 in.	1,542 sq/ft
F-106A	38 ft 3½ in.	70 ft 8¾ in.	20 ft 3¼ in.	631 sq/ft
CV-880	120 ft	129 ft 4 in.	36 ft 3¾ in.	2,000 sq/ft
CV-990A	120 ft	139 ft 9 in.	39 ft 6 in.	2,250 sq/ft
Model 48	27 ft 6 in.	34 ft 10 in.	13 ft 7 in.	216 sq/ft

*Without weather radar
**On skis

Armament

XA-41	Four 0.5 in. Browning machine guns and two 37 mm M-9 cannon in wings and two 500 lb bombs or up to eight machine guns/cannon in multiple combinations and up to 3,200 lb of bombs
XP-81	Six 0.5 in. machine guns or six 20 mm cannon and two 1,600 lb bombs
B-36A/B	72,000 lb bombload
B-36B/D/F/H	Two 20 mm M-24A-1 cannon in six retractable, remote-control fuselage turrets, rear turret and nose position with 9,200 rounds of ammunition and a max bomb load of 86,000 lbs
XB-46	Maximum bomb load of 20,000 lb
YB-60	Two 20 mm cannon in tail and max bomb load of 72,000 lbs
F-102A	Three Hughes AIM-4A or E Falcon semi-active radar-homing missiles and three Hughes AIM-4C or F Falcon infrared homing missiles. Later three Falcons plus one AIM-26A or B. Twenty-four 2.75 in. unguided FFARs
XFY-1	Four 20 mm cannon in wingtip pods or forty-six 2.75 in. unguided rockets
B-58A	One 20 mm T171 cannon and one B53 or four B43 or B61 nuclear bombs
F-106A	One Douglas AIR-2A Genie or AIR-2B Super Genie rocket and four Hughes AIM-4F or AIM-4G Super Falcon air-to-air missiles carried internally. A number of aircraft also had a single 20 mm M61 Vulcan cannon instead of the Genie
Model 48	Four 7.62 mm machine guns and capacity (via hardpoints) to carry up to 2,000 lb in stores

Glossary

AB	Air Base
ACM	Advanced Cruise Missile
ADC	Air Defence Command
ADO	Advanced Development Objective
ADW	Air Defence Wing
AFB	Air Force Base
AFCS	Air Force Communication Service
AGM	Air-to-Ground tactical Missile
AIM	Air Intercept Missile
AMARC	Aircraft Maintenance And Regeneration Centre
AMC	Aviation Manufacturing Corporation
ANG	Air National Guard
ANGB	Air National Guard Base
ARDC	Air Research and Development Command
AVCO	Aviation Corporation
BS	Bomb Squadron
BW	Bomb/Bombardment Wing
CAF	Canadian Armed Forces
CAP	Combat Air Patrol
COIN	Counter Insurgency
DSO	Defence System Operator
ECM	Electronic Counter Measures
EFIS	Electronic Flight Instrument System
FFAR	Forward Firing Aircraft Rocket
FICON	Fighter Conveyor
FIS	Fighter Interceptor Squadron
GE	General Electric
IAF	Indian Air Force
KLM	Koninklijke Luchtvaart Maatschappij
Kw	Kilowatt
LARA	Light Armed Reconnaissance Aircraft
MAD	Magnetic Anomaly Detector
MASDC	Military Aircraft Storage and Disposition Centre
MiG	Mikoyan-Gurevich
NACA	National Advisory Committee of Aeronautics
NAS	Naval Air Station
NASA	National Aeronautics and Space Administration
NATC	Naval Air Test Centre
NEAP	Nuclear Energy for the Propulsion of Aircraft
P&W	Pratt & Whitney

RAAF	Royal Australian Air Force
RAF	Royal Air Force
RCAF	Royal Canadian Air Force
SAGE	Semi-Automatic Guidance Environment
SRG	Strategic Reconnaissance Group
SRW	Strategic Reconnaissance Wing
STOL	Short Take-Off and Landing
USAAC	United States Army Air Corps
USAAF	United States Army Air Force
USAF	United States Air Force
USMC	United States Marine Corps
USN	United States Navy
VJ	Victory in Japan
VTOL	Vertical Take-Off and Landing

Acknowledgements

Many thanks to Debbie Seracini at the San Diego Air & Space Museum for help sourcing a number of photographs and to Bert Ulrich at NASA for assistance with imagery. Also, thank you to Stuart Davidson of JD Transport Collectables for the chance to acquire many of the photographs in this book (Richard L. Ward Collection) and to help build up a new archive on this subject. Special thanks also to my wife Claire, for once again proofing my 'raw' text; I would be lost without you.